Great Cairo
Mother of the World

To
A. M. Stewart

Contents

Preface

IN EXTRICATING THE CONSTANTS and variants in this history of the largest African and Arab city I have been prompted by a purpose which explains the formula of my book. I have wished to make my favorite city known as I myself should like to know, for example, Peking. Knowing little of Chinese history, I should want to be told the most basic information about the strands of information and belief which have woven China. In this spirit I make no apology if I bore, or madden, the expert, if I repeat what is known to him already or explain what he understands. I am writing for potential converts to an interest in Cairo, who may know as little of Egyptian history as I know of Chinese. I am writing for the reader in the armchair as much as for the traveler in the airplane. I hope that the traveler will comprehend better the significance of the city he visits; I hope the reader in the armchair will understand better what he hears of modern Cairo as a result of what he reads.

To make reading easy I have spelled Arabic and Turkish names as simply as possible. My system of transliteration is bound to annoy somebody. Detesting the armory of diacritical signs, I have omitted indications of several Arabic letters which do not exist in English, and which English speakers would mispronounce anyway (for example, the initial *ain* in words like *Ali* and *Aziz*); sometimes I have made indications which are approx-

imate only (as for the terminal ain in the Arabic word for street,
which I have written *sharia*, not *shar'*, as is sometimes done). I
have used the form *al* for the definite article, although the Egyptians (under a French cultural influence) have usually spelled it
el. Where Egyptian names are concerned I have written the Arabic *j* as *g*, since this is how Egyptians pronounce it.

I have made a simple rule about notes. I have used them from
time to time to point a connection between the present and
something or somewhere referred to in the past. Where I name a
source in the text, I leave the interested reader to consult the
bibliography; where I do not, I have inserted a note.

My sources are in large part the illustrious dead. I have
quoted from them gratefully in little and in large. I owe debts to
those who have preserved and edited their works. This debt will
be apparent throughout the book, but I acknowledge it here.

Abdul Latif of Baghdad, whom I quote often, visited Cairo at
the time of Saladin. Ivy E. Videan believes that the spirit of the
long dead physician prompted her and her husband to produce
an edition of his book about Egypt. "Our first meeting with Abd
el-Latif was in August, 1957, when he spoke to my husband
and to me during a conversation with a sensitive, Mrs. Ray
Welch, in London. Since then we have had very many long talks
with him, through Mrs. Welch and also through Mr. Jim Hutch-
ings. It was not unexpected, therefore, that he should tell us in
1960 that he wished my husband to make a photographic copy
of the Bodleian manuscript of the *Kitab al-Ifadah* . . . ." Though
my own conversations with the dead have been less dramatic, I
have found myself haunted in the streets of Cairo by those who
walked them in the past and bequeathed their impressions or
explanations: Nasir Khosrau, the Persian; Ibn Maimun, as the
Arabs know Moses Maimonides; Volney, the Frenchman; Edward Lane, the Englishman; and a host of others.

From the present I draw on experience over almost twenty
years, of which the second decade has been more concentrated
than the first. My connection with Cairo has been of a different
order from the intimate bond that linked me with Baghdad,
where a dozen households made me welcome at all times. During the years 1957 to 1967 Cairo was traversing a period of revolutionary change; the Egyptians, besides, have never displayed
the spectacular hospitality characteristic of the more purely

Arab states. But although I visited fewer houses I received as many impressions and innumerable acts of kindness. I must thank in particular the staff of the Egyptian Geographical Society for their cooperation. Mr. Mahmoud Ali uncovered some little-known Arabic texts and Mr. Muhy Digwy gave me interesting sidelights on the modern Cairo character. In Tangier, Mr. Donald Angus allowed me free run of his considerable library.

1

Mother of the World

Cairo: THE WORLD'S OLDEST monuments in stone mark its
site; the world's longest river pours through its heart. A sphinx
couching among palms, a prostrate pharaoh, recall 'the middle
of the universe,' Memphis, first capital of the Egyptian empire.
The oldest surviving obelisk stands as the sole survival of Heliopolis, twenty miles to the north. Memphis and Heliopolis had
been flourishing for thousands of years when Alexander visited
them; their awe was so potent that the conqueror preferred to
build his Egyptian capital not where the pharaohs had reigned
but on an island joined to Greece by the sea and divided from
Egypt by a lake. Alexandria remained the capital when Augustus made Egypt an imperial province on the death of Cleopatra,
its last Greek sovereign. But under Roman rule, when Egypt
was the granary of the empire, the urban nexus of Memphis and
Heliopolis remained important. The man whom Christians call
the Word of God (the term *Logos* had been coined by philoso-
phers living in Egypt) first spoke words within its purlieus; his
mother washed his linen in a trough inscribed with hieroglyphs.
After being Christian for many centuries, Egypt became a bulwark of Islam in the seventh century. In the Middle Ages this
African city was the largest metropolis in the three continents of
the Old World. Its luxurious way of life, its order and scholar-
ship, impressed visitors from Europe and Asia whose trade

1

passed through its bazaars. As the link between a spiceless West and a remote but luxuriant East, Cairo was rich enough to afford public buildings uniquely splendid.

Its triumph was, however, incomplete and discontinuous. For twenty-five centuries it suffered the indignity of foreign rule: Macedonian kings and Roman prefects, Arabian governors and Turkish sultans, French conquerors and British proconsuls concerned themselves with interests other than those of the people they ruled. The city's prosperity, dependent on a river and a geographical position, could turn to sudden dearth. When the Nile ran low, men died of famine; when in 1498 Vasco da Gama sailed round Africa, Westerners found it possible to reach the Far East without paying Egypt its long-accustomed fee. Under the rule of the Ottoman Turks Cairo had shrunk to a huddle of splendid mosques girt with rubbish hills and evil lakes when Napoleon brought the West to detonate the East. But even then its pyramids inspired his oratory. In a century and a half of consequent effervescence its unique prestige gave it a leading position in the struggle of the Arab and Muslim peoples to throw off Western rule. The opening of the Suez Canal in 1869, the cultivation of cotton, restored it to a position of strategic and commercial power. In the mid-twentieth century, under its first Egyptian ruler since the seventh century BC, it has come to be the voice of those who at once resent and admire the West, the capital not just of Egypt and the Arabs, but the entire Third World.

The fluctuating names of Egypt's capital long puzzled Europeans. John Ogilby, the seventeenth-century English geographer, listed more than a dozen names by which the city had been known to such people as the Chaldeans, Armenians, Hebrews, and Turks. The modern Egyptians use two names when referring to their capital. Each has a meaning and a nuance of its own; both names are used loosely. The first is ancient and popular, the second official and Islamic. Either can refer to the amalgam of towns and cities that have blurred within municipal boundaries which today bind more than 9 million souls. For no one city (unless it be the peripheral village of present-day Memphis) has survived intact or separable from the rest. Each has devoured the past and each has been devoured by its successor. "For this is the practice of kings," wrote a tenth-century Arab,

Maqdisi. "They always efface the traces of their predecessors. This is the prime reason why they destroy cities and fortresses. They did this before Islam, and after it."

The first and most important name is Misr, pronounced more like Musr. This name, far older than the Muslim Arabs, is vague and haunting. Like the Hebrew Mizraim, it refers to the whole country as well as to its capital. Someone who announces: "Tomorrow I travel to Misr," may mean, if he speaks in Paris, that he is going to Egypt; if he speaks in Alexandria, that he is going to Cairo. The sharing of one word for country and capital makes things easier for a writer who would in any case have to interweave the two. It also underlines the extent to which Egypt, since its unification under a first-dynasty pharaoh, has been a centralized state. In no other country in the world, not even France, are the provinces felt to be so provincial; the desert is not felt as being part of Egypt at all. 'Misr' carries with it the attachments of the past, the half-forgotten links with the Memphis and Heliopolis of the pharaohs, with Babylon-in-Egypt, with the earliest cities of Islam. Egyptian peasants are not content with speaking of Misr alone. They expand it to Misr, *um aldunya,* Cairo, mother of the world.

While Misr is timeless, the second name for the city is linked to a date: August 5, AD 969. On that day, in one bold move, a new eastbank capital, an approximate square of about 1200 yards each way, was pegged out by a conquering general. The astrologers in whom the general reposed his trust

> consulted together to determine the auspicious moment for the opening ceremony. Bells were hung on ropes from pole to pole, and at the signal of the sages their ringing was to announce the precise moment when the labourers were to turn the first sod. The calculations of the astrologers were, however, anticipated by a raven, who perched on one of the ropes and set the bells jingling, upon which every mattock was struck into the earth, and the trenches were opened. It was an unlucky hour: the planet Mars (in Arabic, al-Qahir) was in the ascendant; but it could not be undone, and the place was accordingly named after the hostile planet, al-Qahira,[1] the 'martial' or 'triumphant,' in the hope that the sinister omen might be turned to a triumphant issue.[2]

The general's city, the first true Cairo, had its epithet also: 'the Guarded.' This originally derived from the high walls that hedged it in. On Egyptian lips it came to include an implicit prayer against the baleful planet that had presided at the city's birth.

Mother of the world, the Guarded: such Arabic hyperbole has echoed from Morocco to Kuwait. It has annoyed non-Arabs. Writing when Constantinople ruled the Ottoman empire (and in theory Egypt), the Turkish poet Fazil Bey retorted: "Misr, mother of the world? She is only a whore who has given herself up to the world each century."

The Arabic phrase 'mother of the world,' *um al-dunya,* has the same force as those German compounds that begin with *ur.* Cairo (used loosely to include all the cities on this site) is the *Urstadt,* the primordial city. In the same way Muslim theologians speak of a 'mother of the Book,' a primordial scripture laid up in Heaven from which both Bible and Koran derive. Cairo's stresses and pains, its triumphs and problems, cut a stencil which fits the experience of later cities. Most cities are, indeed, later. When Constantinople was being founded the southern tip of the Egyptian delta had already witnessed a formidable history of urban living. The earliest city on this site, the Memphis of the pharaohs, antedates almost every other human conglomerate larger than a village; as an imperial capital it antedates them all.

Cities were themselves the spoor of a new kind of man. For unnumbered millennia human beings had wandered in search of their food; in tribal migrations they followed the animal tribes they hunted or the berries and fruits that flourished in different places in different seasons. Such nomadic peoples would sometimes build forts or permanent structures to which they would periodically return. But the settled village became a necessity when cereals began to be cultivated; the village houses, huddled together, guarded the fields and the corn which the fields produced. As such villages multiplied—their traces have been found, among other places, in Anatolia, Kurdistan, the Indus valley—villages joined together in common defense against the remaining nomads or alien groups. Primitive Egypt, a land of marshy thickets thronged with wild fowl, was divided into two such states: in the north, the delta; in the south, the valley stretching from the delta's apex to the first cataract at Aswan. Each of these states had its own capital and its local gods. Around 3000 BC the two states, Lower and Upper Egypt, were linked into one great kingdom. Its capital was founded about fifteen miles from the heart of modern Cairo.

In building where they did, the builders of Memphis showed strategic sense. They built on the west bank of the Nile. At that time the delta—whose southern apex is pushed approximately one mile north every five hundred years—started to fan out where Memphis now is. (The point of the delta is now more than ten miles north of Cairo.)

The strategic motives that inspired the choice of site are as evident today (taking into account the changes of the river and the retreat of the delta) as when those first engineers set their men to work.

There are geographical constants which time has hardly touched. These constants accoumpany the Nile on its northward journey from the granite islands that form the first cataract at Aswan. There are variants which, like the thematic variations in an Arab musical theme, surround a monotonous core. This central monotone, these slight variations, can be seen from an airplane flying from the south. For five hundred miles the Nile follows a natural rift through limestone hills. Some seasons the color of the water is reddish brown; at other times it takes the greenish hue after which dressmakers have named their *eau-de-Nil*. The cliffs, now approaching, now drawing back, maintain an average of ten miles' fertile soil; this is *kemi*, the 'black land' of the early Egyptians. The 'red land,' *toshri*, or desert, seen from above, shows the brainlike whorls of convoluted bluffs, savage and bare. Sometime, long ago, the wild mountains were worn away by tributaries whose ghosts are flattened wadis where freak storms even now may cause tidal floods. This flatter earth resembles a photograph of a beach enlarged by an instrument as tall as the Eiffel Tower.

And then after this momentous passage—flights of geese or stands of palm make the monotony a delight to the traveler on the river or on the ground—there begins to be a change. The enclosing hills[3] move farther apart; and then, as a twenty-mile stretch of pyramids appears to the west, the hills abruptly change direction as though they were teams of horses obeying a

6

circus master's whip. Instead of running parallel with the northward-pushing Nile they pivot west-northwest and east-northeast, allowing the river to flow broad and free. To the east, a broken line of beige and khaki cliffs are the Mokattam heights; they rise 550 feet above the Nile; their stormworn, eroded cliffs once overlooked the Mediterranean, before the delta had begun to form, when the Nile poured its Congo water and its Ethiopian silt deep into the sea. The western hills, the Libyan plateau, are the start of the Sahara. As the two groups of hills swerve from the river, the Nile is constrained no more. The artery of Egypt has changed into an intricate web of capillaries and veins. The slim growth which ran beside the artery's banks turns into a vast open fan. In color the fields are emerald green; yet they shimmer with the evaporation from the little canals which make the green possible, which permit the heavy-sailed feluccas to navigate from one up-piled village to another in a landscape that seems limitlessly rich until, if the plane persists on its northern flight, the green merges with the sea.

The Greeks compared the rich part of Egypt not to an opened fan, but to the fourth letter of their alphabet written in capital form with its base facing north toward them: ∇. The delta might also be compared to an open hand, to one of those signs for good luck which the Muslims were to inherit from the past. Where Cairo stands is the pulse, the wrist. Whosoever controls this pulse can control both the valley and the delta: the men from the south, who make trouble or, when properly trained, control it; and the men of the north, whose agricultural wealth makes the country worth controlling. The Nile is not the only route controlled by this point. Northeast from Cairo, skirting the Mokattam hills, a broad waterless valley, the Wadi Tumilat, leads to the Isthmus of Suez. Caravans following this natural road could thus link Egypt with the Red Sea and the land route to Palestine.

Other ancient cities were built with a similar regard to controlling agriculture and territory. Ur and Babylon guarded the river system of Iraq. But the Tigris and Euphrates were less cooperative rivers than the Nile.

"The Nile increases," a twelfth-century Arab was to write,[4] "when all other rivers diminish and their waters are lowest, because it begins to rise at the moment when the days are longest in summer and finishes its rise at the autumn equinox." This convenient flood was linked with the Nile's direction of flow from the tropical south to the moderate north, from the uplands of Ethiopia and the jungles of the Congo where rain falls in summer. The Tigris and Euphrates flowed south from the uplands of Asia Minor and Iran. The melting snows of the northern spring would pound south at a time when Mesopotamia had no particular need of water; they could cause floods of the enormity described in Genesis. When summer began to parch the land both rivers were tame and low; there was no easy way of storing water.

Cairo's position on the Nile was no less strategic than that of Troy, built on narrows through which ships from the Black Sea brought corn to the Greek archipelago. Troy persisted through sixteen lives; but wars, earthquakes, and political change achieved its final and post-Homeric death. From Roman times until the nineteenth century Troy was a silent hillock where goats clambered through the winds.

Cairo guards more than a breadbasket and a strategic pulse-point. It dominates a waterway far easier to navigate than the Euphrates or the Dardanelles.

To this day uneducated Egyptians refer to their river as *al-bahr*, or 'the sea'; and this was the first sea on which men learned to sail. Apart from being sheltered, the Nile as a sea, had two advantages. Its constant tide was from the south to the north. Its dominant wind was in the opposite direction. The man who wished to travel north from the first cataract had merely to launch a raft upon the Nile and the impetus of the river would carry him and his goods as far as he wished to go. And the man who wished to journey to the south did not need to fight the current with oars. A strong and persistent wind blew steadily south. It made the up-river journey, against the stream, easy for any craft with sails. (The same wind alleviated the Egyptian summers. From earliest times until today the people of the country have sought to place their houses so that the windows catch a breeze as pleasing to the settled as it is useful to the sailor.)

When the capital at the tip of the delta grew, when its resources and its need expanded, its central position could be exploited further. Caravan routes to the east would be followed by man-made waterways making it possible to ship goods from the Nile to the Red Sea.

A city lulled in too much convenience would die of a yawn if its citizens, were not first clubbed to death like drunken seals.

Part of the stencil which this primordial city cuts is one of dialogue with nature, sometimes of violent dispute. Such disputes stimulate like good arguments—unless one of the parties loses his temper, takes to arms, and kills. When a city's dispute with nature is unfairly balanced, the city may be destroyed. An earthquake or a flood may destroy it forever.

Cairo's dispute has been with water, the humblest and strongest of elements. It has been a dispute in which need has been balanced by dread and in which the Nile has often repaired the catastrophes it has itself caused.

All those who have built on this site—pharaohs, kings, governors, caliphs, sultans, slaves, and beys—have had a double preoccupation: their city must be near enough the Nile for its water to be freely available; at the same time houses had to be high enough above the river bank to escape the engulfing floods which were the occasional counterpart to drought.

The Nile has not only pushed its delta forward in the last millennia, it has also constantly changed its course. While in Pharaonic times it had had a pronounced westward bend, in later centuries it deposited more and more of its agglutinative silt toward the east, so that in historical times the channel has moved contantly farther from the Mokattam hills, enlarging the area of cultivable or habitable land. The Nile's silt was so cohesive that it would cohere round any stable object, such as a wrecked ship, and begin, quite quickly, to compose an island. There are at the moment two considerable inhabited islands: Gezira to the north, and Roda to the south. Gezira is comparatively new. Roda has moved steadily north over the centuries; its southern tip was once its northern limit. At the same time the channel between Roda and the eastern bank of the Nile has tended to grow narrower, making the provision of water for the thousands living on the east bank constantly more difficult. A canal which the pharaohs had designed to link the Nile with the Red Sea would become in medieval times an instrument for bringing water into the heart of Cairo, from whose walls the river had progressively withdrawn. Throughout the centuries this canal (in Arabic, *al-Khalig al-Misri,* the canal of Misr) was kept dammed until the height of summer, when its breaching was the secular feast of the year. The dry canal would then flow with water which for three pleasant months would be clear and sweet; after November it would be stagnant and smelly; it would then become a dry ditch of rats and refuse until in August it would be filled again.

Only in the early twentieth century were the upper reaches of the Nile itself to be dammed, for flood control and storage. Until then the annual supply of water was entirely dependent on the rains in Ethiopia and the Congo basin, or what the Egyptians fancied were springs in the Mountains of the Moon. No measures to bring the Nile water nearer the capital, no system of canals, was any use if there was not enough water to bring. There was no way of storing water in a sodden year for use in a year of drought. The wells which filled after the annual flood lasted some months but were brackish and drinkable only in an emergency. The fields which were watered by one annual inundation depended on a flood large enough to overflow the banks.

If the ruler could not control the amount of water, he could, by the use of measuring instruments, estimate from the level of the annual flood the agricultural prospects for the coming year. Since at least 3600 BC the height of the Nile flood was recorded annually as the major statistic of the year. The Pharaonic priests had devised the first Nilometers; the Copts had maintained their secrets; and the Arabs learned from them. The southern tip of Roda island was the site of the city's chief Nilometer, an instrument marked out in cubits, a measure based on the distance from the elbow to the tip of the middle finger.

> Upon another side of the island standeth a house alone by itself, in the midst whereof there is a foursquare cistern or channel of eighteen cubits deep, whereinto the water of Nilus is conveyed by a certain sluice under the ground. And in the midst of the cistern there is erected a certain pillar, which is marked and divided into so many cubits as the cistern itself containeth in depth. And upon the 17th June when Nilus beginneth to overflow, the water thereof conveyed by the said sluice into the channel, increaseth daily, sometimes two and sometimes three fingers, and sometimes half a cubit in height. Unto this place there

daily resort certain officers appointed by the senate, who viewing and observing the increase of Nilus, declare unto certain children how much it hath increased, which children wearing yellow scarfs upon their heads, do publish the said increase of Nilus in every street of the city and the suburbs, and receive gifts every day of the merchants, artificers and women, so long as Nilus increaseth.

This account of the Nilometer and the public interest in the Nile was written in the sixteenth century by Leo Africanus, a Moor converted to the Christian faith; it would have been equally true at any time until the twentieth century.

The Nile rose between its banks, then overflowed them, during the astrological signs of Cancer, Leo, and Virgo. Its waters spilled out over all the cultivated land in the valley and the delta. Receding, they left behind a glutinous deposit of silt which was then ploughed and sown.

For Egypt to avoid the twin perils of flood and drought the Nile had to rise between limits known to all. If it rose more than twenty cubits, higher ground was invaded, houses overwhelmed, and stagnant lakes were formed; the water did not recede from the lower ground in time and was thus without use for crops. Such high floods were rare. For an excellent harvest an ideal level was eighteen cubits. Anything between twenty cubits and sixteen would provide enough food to last two years. It was therefore important for the country's rulers to estimate the future. If there were signs of coming dearth, precautions could be taken in advance. If there were signs of coming bounty, plans for storage could be made.

The rulers were particularly preoccupied with the vegetation on which they and their subjects lived; they were less concerned with the water their subjects drank. The aqueducts built by various rulers were to carry water for palace or citadel. Not until the early nineteenth century was an aqueduct used to bring water for general use. The city's needs for clean water were always great. They were keenest in summer, when May to July was torrid and July to October humid from the flood. These needs were met by an army of water carriers as highly organized as London taxi drivers but enjoying higher popular esteem.

"From water all that lives . . . ." The Koranic phrase with which the water seller (or *saqi*) would salute his client expressed the pride of a respected if ill-rewarded caste. (As late as 1830 the *saqi* earned a penny for carrying one of his huge skins full of water a mile and a half.) Since all life not only came from water but depended on it, the *saqi* was a benefactor of the city. He had many colleagues. A traveler of the fourteenth century (not, admittedly, a century of precise statistics) estimated that 12,000 employed camels and another 30,000 employed mules.

The water sellers were governed by an intricate accumulation of laws and customs. They must not draw water from places contaminated by sewage or the outflow of slaughterhouses; they must avoid stagnant pools. In order to qualify for this profession, a British traveler wrote in the 1690s an apprentice must carry a skin weighing sixty-seven pounds for three days and nights without a pause. Once enrolled, the *saqi* had to be ready to play the role of municipal fireman; to assist him in this work, a law required householders to keep Ali Baba–sized jars filled to the top with water in case of fire.

Every prosperous household had its cistern, which was constantly refilled. Like a modern tradesman, the *saqi* kept careful note of his account: he either scratched figures on his clients' doors, or used a string of blue beads, ticking one off for each skin of water.

The poor could not afford cisterns of their own. It was therefore considered a pious act to endow a public cistern, or sebeel. The public cistern would often occupy the ground floor of a two-story building. Here behind intricately fretted grilles the poor women of the quarter would fetch water free; here they would gossip with the *saqis*, who besides being benefactors of the city were famous go-betweens, having a right of entry to houses denied to other males. Above the cistern, on the second floor, would be a school. Here boys would rock back and forth on their heels as they memorized the scriptures of Islam. As water for the body, so religion for the soul.

Animals were not neglected. One hot day the Prophet Muhammad had seen a harlot using her slipper to scoop up water for a dog. "For this action," he had proclaimed, "you will enter paradise." Troughs for animals (including the camels and mules of the water sellers) stood outside mosques.

The *saqi* had an honored place in the major religious occasion of the year: the pilgrimage to Mecca. Without him and his supplies the journey could not take place. He was also a target of war. Anyone who wished to invest the city on the high ground to the east of the Nile would try to cut it off from its water supply. In 1711, for example, a body of Turkish soldiers combined with Bedouin Arabs against the citizens of the town. Their tactics were not to assault Saladin's walls (which were never carried by storm) but to occupy the places opposite Roda Island where the water sellers filled their skins. Cut off from the Nile, Cairo could not long survive.

Primordial in its strategic site, primordial in its dialogue with nature, Cairo has epitomized urban life in showing how a mature city produces citizens of a recognizable mold. This mold is shaped by the city's hinterland and its people's experience.

Cairo's hinterland is complex. It combines the narrow Nile valley, the rich Nile delta, and the vast expanse of encompassing desert. A city where farmers sell their crops, a city where bureaucrats tax and judge the farmers, a city where travelers meet, it has been a cosmopolis with a history sometimes jubilant and often harrowing.

Though their shrouds preserve less than their buildings, though their words and deeds are forgotten by their heirs, men and women are the most interesting results of the civilizations they build. Observers have been summing up the Cairenes for centuries. Ibn Redwan, physician to an eleventh-century caliph, found them "greedy, avaricious, idle, timid, lying, given over to intrigues." Another added to these adjectives "mercurial, indecisive and given to swift change of mind." Yet in one of their worst periods, the sixteenth century, Leo Africanus saw them in a more kindly light: "They are of good company, leading amusing lives, fast to promise yet slow to effect; few of them study; their women disdain to spin, sew or cook; their husbands have to buy the meat ready cooked; their households are disunited."

The product of this city, the Cairene, is in a sense the hero, sometimes antihero, of this book: what he did, what he made, what others did to him. But one primordial problem of all cities can, without fear of putting the last first, be abstracted here.

Since man is often violent when strong and malicious when weak, the first problem of a city where thousands rub shoulders is the problem of violence. Unless the fact of living together in the human equivalent of an ant hill modifies human nature, the city falls into anarchy and chaos. Young cities can sometimes afford violence; they have the energy to rebuild. They often cannot avoid it: their citizens have not learned to cohere. But violence is something that cities must tame if they are to survive.

The solution of the problem of violence in Cairo has been difficult. The Egyptian stock is sturdy, in particular when it derives from the south. Sudden rages can be fired by a hot, dry climate. As long ago as the age of Constantine an observer complained that "the Egyptians showed an appetite for quarrel and strife and unparalleled deceit and litigiousness, not only to their superiors, but also among themselves. These otherwise gloomy people would then be seen aflame with fiery anger and wild insults, perhaps only because a greeting had not been returned, or place had not been yielded in the baths, or because their insane vanity had otherwise been injured."[5] The novelist Tawfik al-Hakim, who spent many years as a country prosecutor, marveled at the capacity of the Egyptian peasant to lose his head over women and over land. Rancor could express itself in killing neighbors or burning their crops.

The interaction of this basic violence with the congestion of Cairo has produced a remarkable solution: a folk ballet of violence, the *dowshah*.

Almost any visitor to Cairo may expect to witness a *dowshah*. It may erupt beneath his hotel window; it may be in progress as he visits a bazaar; or at any street corner, by any stall for nuts or cigarettes, its peculiar staccato sound may suddenly be heard.

There is no need to write a modern description. This ritual of defused violence has been noticed through the centuries. Leonardo Frescobaldi, a prosperous fourteenth-century Florentine, arrived in Egypt from an Italy where all men carried swords. He first marveled that "the Egyptians are scarcely the warrior type and do not carry weapons." He then went on to give a classic account of what happens in a *dowshah*:

> When they begin to quarrel the onlooker expects them to tear each other to pieces. But the moment one of them cries *Istafurla*, which in their language means 'Peace for God's sake!' they at once calm down.

Leo Africanus, whose description of the Nilometer has already been given, describes, two centuries after Frescobaldi, the *dowshah* in similar terms:

> And if any of them chance to fall out in the streets, they presently go to buffets, and then a great number of people come flocking about them to see the conflict, and will not depart thence, till they have reconciled them.

In other, newer, cities trivial incidents—the arrest of a dangerous driver, interference with children splashing in a hydrant—have set off destructive riots. Cairo is too old, too fragile, too combustible, for such riots to be tolerable. The Cairene's experience has been of violence from others; against it he tends to shut his doors and pull his quilt over his eyes.

Modern annals offer one exception. On January 26, 1952, an organized mob destroyed cinemas, cabarets, and hotels associated with the power then occupying Egypt. But the cause was not trivial. The previous day, in the Canal Zone, a large number of Egyptian policemen, ordered by their government to resist the British, were shot dead on their own land by foreigners. The Cairo police refused to support a system which had permitted this to happen. They did nothing to stop a riot which expressed the despair of a city without hope.

The *dowshah* deserves applause. It is an institution for the relief of tension which could arise only in a city with a millennial past. Cairo has ruled an empire comprising most of the known world; it has been a provincial city in a Greco–Roman province, the awesome powerhouse of a caliphate, the leave center of European armies. Its people, having seen and remembered a great deal, have learned the lesson that serious violence brings a bitter harvest. Violence of emotion cannot be abolished by law. It can be sublimated in a ritual pantomime. The vile words fly, the fierce fists are raised. But when "a great number of people come flocking about them," the contestants will, with a great show of reluctance, with fists held back as though against bands of steel, allow themselves to be parted, so that, till the next disturbance, the street is calm—or calm but for its daily sound: the cries of vendors, the hurly-burly of traffic, and the oaths of men exaggerating in the name of God.

2

Memphis and Heliopolis

T<small>HE CARDINAL EVENT IN EGYPTIAN HISTORY</small>—the event as a
result of which Egypt was to influence the world—was the act
whereby the southern valley and the northern delta were linked
in one state. This act has been traditionally ascribed to Menes,
an Upper Egyptian who lived approximately 3500 years before
Christ. The new unity was symbolized by the god–king, or
pharaoh, who wore the high conical crown of the south and the
complex, high-backed crown of the north, and who reigned from
his new capital at Memphis, a city built precisely where delta
and valley met.

The Greek historian Herodotus visited Egypt in the fifth century BC, when the unification was as distant in time from him
as he is from us. He obtained his story from the living reposito-
ries of Egyptian tradition:

> The priests informed me that Menes, who first ruled
> over Egypt, started by protecting Memphis with a
> mound; for the whole river formerly ran close to the
> sandy mountains on the side of Libya; but Menes, be-
> ginning about a hundred stades above Memphis, filled
> in the elbow towards the south, dried up the old chan-
> nel, and conducted the river into a canal, so as to make
> it flow between the two mountain ridges: this bed of
> the Nile, which flows excluded from its original course,

is still carefully upheld by the Persians, being made secure every year; for if the river should break through and overflow in this part, there would be danger lest all Memphis should be flooded.

The purpose of Menes was twofold. The original river bed now provided flattened and fertile ground for a city of small mud-brick houses with gardens; at the same time the new city was protected from the east (the source of most attacks in Egyptian history) by the whole stream of the Nile. Before he diverted the river in this huge operation there had been insufficiency of ground on the west bank for a capital of the grandeur he envisaged.

A further reason has been advanced by an English hydrologist.[1] The western bend would have encouraged silting. Since the Egyptians depended on the Nile for transport and drinking water, it was important that "towns should be established on an outward bend where no silting—such as would be probable on an inner bend—would be likely to take place."

The achievement of Menes was to be a great deal more lasting than the work of most town planners. For many thousand years Memphis was to be either the capital of Egypt or its second city. Its tutelary deity, described as "the creator of the gods and of the world," was Ptah, whose temple was the most imposing building in a city commonly known as Hat-ka-Ptah, Place of the Soul of Ptah. This creative god was portrayed as a bearded man clad in close-fitting white garments, his feet joined together as though he were mummified. His head was usually bare, though in later times he was shown in a variety of royal crowns. His complexion was shown as pale yellow, a color often reserved for foreigners in ancient Egyptian art; but it is likely that in the case of Ptah a lack of sunburn is intended to show his reflective, intellectual nature, fitting a god who stayed diligently in his workshop. The Greeks easily identified Ptah with their own Hephaestus, the artificer of Olympus. But there was more to Ptah than creativity. He was shown standing on a pedestal which was later interpreted as the hieroglyph of justice. One text survives in which a man smitten by blindness sees in his fate the punishment for perjury and implores the god's forgiveness:

I am one who swore falsely by Ptah, the Lord of
　　Justice;
He made me see darkness in daytime.
I shall tell his power to the one who knoweth him not,
　　as well as to the one who knoweth,
To the small and to the great.
Beware of Ptah, the Lord of Justice!

Memphis was the capital of an empire whose power was to affect its neighbors and whose lure as a commercial center was to
draw merchandise from Crete and Lebanon to the great stone
wharfs that lined the Nile. But except for the temples, a citadel
known as the White Wall, and the city and harbor walls, Memphis was put together from the same sun-dried bricks as form
the houses of the fellahin in the villages of Sakkara, Mit-rahina,
and Abusir which today mark the site of the ancient capital.
The mud houses of Pharaonic times have long since returned to
the Nile silt from which they came, while the public and royal
buildings have been digested in cannibalistic greed by the capitals which have arisen across the river on the eastern bank.

The process has been continuously destructive.

As late as AD 1200 an Arab traveler[2] could muse on the un-
told wonders of this ruined city. One wonder which was not destroyed until 1449 was

> the building called the Green Building. It is made from
> one vast block of stone nine cubits high and eight long
> and seven wide. In the midst of this stone a room has
> been hollowed out; it is formed by leaving two cubits
> thickness to the side walls as well as the floor and
> roof. Inside and out it is completely covered with reliefs
> and paintings and hieroglyphic inscriptions. Outside
> there are designs of the morning sun as well as stars,
> spheres, men and beasts. The men are shown in vari-
> ous postures. Some standing, some walking, some with
> a leg stretched forward, some at rest. Some of them
> have hitched up their clothes for working; some are car-
> rying things; some are giving orders concerned with the
> work.

This remarkable shrine stood in a magnificent temple made of
cyclopean stones, fitted neatly together.

Even then vandals were at work. The Green Building had been undermined by seekers for buried treasure; the single block from which it was made was already cracked. The astonished visitor noted "one statue of very large dimensions from the scalp of which a millstone had been cut, two cubits in diameter, without being greatly deformed by the excision, or even showing much evident change." Where temples were bound together by metal links, "vile and wretched individuals have sought after these bands of copper and torn away a considerable quantity. In order to get them they have smashed a number of stones."

Nor were the vandals always petty thieves. The Green Building was to be destroyed by an important prince.[3] The vandals often had exalted motives. They took columns by the thousand for their own newer shrines on the other bank.

Time and its agents were to be even more destructive of Heliopolis, the City of the Sun, which was the second Pharaonic foundation near the apex of the Delta, the site of modern Cairo. All that remains of Heliopolis today is an obelisk of the twelfth dynasty (around 1900 BC), a symbol of solar worship.

Heliopolis was the religious center of ancient Egypt. Standing on slightly raised ground to the east of the delta, in dry air where the power of the sun was visibly potent, this city contained the elements of a cult behind the cults, a system of ideas underlying the worship of birds, beasts, insects, and intellectual abstractions. Its center was a spring of fresh water known to this day as the Spring of the Sun.[4] In this sacred well "the sun was believed either to bathe himself morning and night or to have been born at the beginning of the world, when he arose from the abyss."[5] Another object of reverence was the holy Persea, a large lauraceous tree considered the foremost earthly proxy of the Tree of Heaven.

The Tree of Heaven illustrates, as a concept, the beauties and the confusions of the Pharaonic faith. The notion itself shines with poetic power. The chief of the gods was supposed to inscribe the names of the living on its leaves. The Persea had many different types of tree proxies, growing in different shrines; this various abundance shows the pleasant confusion of Egyptian beliefs, each merging in the next. Sometimes the proxy would be a sycamore, the Egyptian tree with the widest-spreading branches; sometimes a lofty date palm; sometimes the cedar growing in the mountains of Lebanon, a Pharaonic dependency; sometimes the vine, identified with Osiris, the god of death and rebirth. Or because the willow grew near water—the spring at Heliopolis was an earthly prototype of the Osirian abyss from which life began—the willow too could be an earthly type of the transcendental tree.

The priests of Heliopolis made an early attempt to systematize beliefs which in their nature were unsystematic, to reconcile gods who were originally the competing deities of villages and towns. Their greatest achievement, dating to roughly the same period as the founding of Memphis, was the isolation of an 'ennead,' or genealogy of nine gods. The primal god was the sun (known sometimes as Atum, the primitive deity of Heliopolis, more often as Re) from whom descended in the third generation two couples, Osiris and his sister–wife Isis, and the baleful Seth and his sister Nephthys. Despite this gallant attempt, Pharaonic theologians never produced a coherent or consistent creed.

The greatest religious reformer of the Pharaonic religion was Akhnaton, the fourteenth-century BC pharaoh whose short-lived capital was halfway between Memphis and the southern capital of Thebes. For reasons which have been variously interpreted, Akhnaton advocated the cult of one god only, the sun-disc Aton. But even the priests of Heliopolis, within a conservative tradition, reached through sun worship something akin to the conception of one force animating all. Because of the fluidity of Egyptian thought—so alien to the fixed categories of Europe—it was possible for a priest in an eighth-century BC papyrus to argue that Ptah was himself the antecedent of all the gods, the begetter, through a form of himself, of the sun itself. Ptah is "he who standeth on the earth and toucheth the sky with his head, he whose upper half is the sky and whose lower half is the underworld." This god can change his name to Amen-Re (a synthesis of the local god of Thebes with the solar god of Heliopolis) and at the same time represent the cosmos manifesting itself in plural forms and names:

> Thy forms are Nile and Earth,
> Thou art the eldest, greater than the gods.
> Thou art the abyss when it stretched itself over the
>   ground;

Thou didst return in thy ripples.
Thou art the sky, thou art the earth, thou art the un-
derworld,
Thou art the water, thou art the air between them.

The metaphysics of the Egyptian priests, to whom cult was
more important than belief, moved by intuitive analogies rather
than by logic; these analogies could be profound when the intuit-
ing minds were still poetic. With the passage of time they
turned to meaningless spells. As religion they were to yield before the incisive monotheism of the Semitic peoples to the east,
as philosophy they were to yield before the organized thinking of
the Greeks from the north. But in one important aspect they
were to remain visible to the eye and influential to the heart.

More than any other people in history the ancient Egyptians
were obsessed with death. Delighting in the pleasures of this
world, they sought through the mechanism of their liturgy and
magic to ensure their continuation in the next. They believed
this could be done through mummifying the body and preserving
it in a lasting house. The people of Memphis and Heliopolis built
houses for eternity which have remained to this day.

Behind Memphis on the Sakkara ridge, to the west of Cairo
and Heliopolis on the Giza plateau, are the great burial grounds
of the pharaohs and their subjects. Tombs have been preserved
by sheer size or concealing sand.

Overlooking the mud-brick houses and dusty date palms of
modern Memphis stands the first great architectural monument
in stone[6] to be built on the planet Earth: an oblong step pyramid within whose entrails lies a mastaba, a square building
250 feet on each side and 25 feet high. Such mastabas (so
named by Arab excavators in the nineteenth century because
they resembled the mastabas—or benches—on which they sat
outside their homes) covered deep shafts in which the coffins of
the dead were laid. (The Sakkara shaft is 104 feet deep and
leads to a subterranean gallery 97 feet long.) Imhotep, a scien-
tist of such genius that he was later deified as the god of healing
and identified by the Greeks with Aesculapius, worked for
Zoser, a third-dynasty pharaoh of the twenty-eighth century BC.
Imhotep recognized that his master's mastaba, set in a huge
courtyard with high walls, would be invisible from Memphis on
the plain below. He therefore erected above it, first a four- then a

six-tier structure, 195 feet high, the first pyramid in Egypt or the world. It has been well described as "a gigantic flight of steps reaching up towards the sky, which would enable the soul of the dead king to ascend towards the sun, his father Re."[7] This building, at once gigantic and simple, still dominates both the western skyline and the ruins of its own walled courtyard. In one part of this courtyard Zoser would run a ceremonial race in honor of Apis, the divine bull. This cult of Apis once again displayed the liquidity of Egyptian beliefs, as well as their evident origins in an agricultural society. A particular bull—black with certain white marks resembling an eagle's wings on his forehead and back—was 'discovered' by the priests in a manner that recalls the selection of a Tibetan Dalai Lama. Each new sacred bull was supposed to have been conceived by a ray of sunlight on a cow. In his lifetime he was honored as 'Ptah renewing himself'; the way he ate his food, the paths he chose, were taken as oracles. When he died he was mourned for seventy days, embalmed and buried in a giant sarcophagus, its granite brought by raft from Aswan.

As well as pharaohs and bulls, lesser mortals were buried by the thousand round the step pyramid of Sakkara and the yet larger fourth-dynasty pyramids of Giza to the north. Bas-reliefs on the walls of such tombs embodied the delights and comforts which the dead hoped to enjoy in the hereafter; magic formulae empowered the dead to pass into immortal bliss.

The Egyptian attitude to death has sent tentacles of influence through time and space, influencing Christianity through Plato, himself a visitor to Heliopolis. The influence persists in modern Cairo, whose burial customs are unique in the Islamic world. To the east of the clangorous city is a vast duplicate: little houses with doors and windows line roads which differ from ordinary streets only in their silence and lack of traffic. These are the houses for eternity of today's Egyptians. Each well-to-do Cairo family has such a house. Inside are what look like rooms. Under the floors in crypts are laid out the family dead, the men in one crypt, the women in another. Here as in ancient times relatives come to visit the dead on the great religious occasions of the year. There is one difference, however. In ancient times it was important for the *ka*, the dead person's soul, to be offered flowers to smell and food to eat. At the same time it was vital for the dead body to be far below ground to avoid robbers. The art of sculpture arose as a response to the need for surrogate figures for the safely buried. In a ground-level funerary chapel a lifelike statue would stand waiting to receive visits and gifts. The living could in this way make contact with the inviolate dead. Muslims, praying only to God and giving only to the poor, and in a Semitic tradition hostile to representational art, have produced no sculpture worthy of the name.

There was a poetic balance in the two important cities on the opposite banks of the Nile but within easy reach of each other near this stratigic site: Memphis, on the west bank to the south, was dedicated to Ptah and the practical tasks of power; Heliopolis, or On, on the east bank to the north, was dedicated to the sun god, Amen-Re, and the metaphysics of Egyptian'life. The tension between the two kept Egyptian society alive through the long ages when few challengers from outside threatened the authority of Pharaoh. Even when the challenges began to multiply, the balanced harmony of Memphis and Heliopolis were to impress and change the bringers of challenge.

3

Babylon-in-Egypt

After producing more than thirty dynasties whose average span was at least as long as the United States' existence as a nation, after responding to countless challenges, Pharaonic civilization was to respond no more. Its central spirit, that nexus of interwoven forces which gives a society its distinctive traits, had grown tired; its creative impetus had cooled. Designs which had been fresh and individual at Sakkara degenerated into the stereotyped motifs of the decorator. They had been repeeated so often that they turned into the trumpery postcards of religious art, stylized conventions produced by the square yard and without power to move. The gods of the pharaohs were no longer prayed to with belief; the analogies no longer made sense; the priests were trusted no more. Foreigners created the later dynasties. Libyans from the west, Nubians from the south, then Persians from the east invaded the rich valley, interested in wealth and indifferent to the lot of those who produced it. Yet to the end those who conquered Egypt put on its impressive clothes, adopted its ancient rituals, and bowed to its mysterious gods; they took their place in a hierarchic system whose immense age gave it still a sort of power.

When the Persians occupied Memphis in the late sixth century BC, they brought with them, according to one tradition, a host of workmen from Babylon on the Euphrates. These Persian pharaohs were to complete the canal which the fifteenth-dynasty pharaoh Necho had begun in 609 BC. Necho's waterway followed much the same route east through the Wadi Tumilat as a canal which had existed seven centuries earlier in the reign of Seti I. Near where the canal branched northeast from the Nile the Persians built a fortress on the heights of al-Rasad, a spur of the Mokattam. Near this eastbank fortress (commanding a wesward view of Memphis and the pyramids which lined the Libyan escarpment) a new city was to grow up. Different traditions account for its name, Babylon-in-Egypt. According to one, the Chaldean workmen, exhausted by harsh treatment, rose in revolt and, crossing from Memphis, seized the fortress and its surrounding site. Granted an amnesty, they were allowed to settle where they were and build a town. By the waters of Memphis the Chaldeans remembered their Euphrates home. They called their settlement 'Babylon-in-Egypt.'

Another theory derives the name from an entirely different root. Babylon, in this theory, is a corruption of Bab-li-On, meaning the Gate to On. On was the biblical name for Heliopolis; the new city was certainly placed at the southern extremity of the straggling religious ancient one.

Whatever the origins of its name, the city occupied a newly strategic site. After Menes had diverted the Nile to build his west-bank capital, the apex of the delta had moved steadily north. Other changes in the river and the world gave new importance to the east bank. One was the emergence of the considerable island of Roda, lying like a flounder immediately to the west of the heights of al-Rasad. Roda was separated from the east bank (as it is today) by a narrow channel; this channel could be bridged by linked boats and from the west bank of Roda the task of traversing the other half of the Nile was considerably less. Babylon's proximity to Roda gave it an easy link to Memphis and the west; its proximity to the canal (an intermittently functioning thoroughfare from the time of Darius until the early Middle Ages) linked Babylon with an east grown richer and more developed since the time when Memphis had been planned.

Babylon's Persian nucleus was to develop into the chief Egyptian (as opposed to foreign) city during the thousand years in which Greek influence dominated Egypt.

The Greeks had always been aware of the wealth of Egypt. Cretan sailors had docked at the Memphis wharfs; Helen, according to one tale, had landed in Egypt after the fall of Troy. Herodotus had recorded the peculiarities of the Egyptians for his Hellenic readers: it was the only country where women urinated standing up, he claimed, and where men performed the same office sitting down.On a more serious level, he had gossiped with the priests of On. From the same priests Plato had learned the story of Atlantis. According to a modern theory, he got the Pharaonic numerals wrong, thus siting Atlantis too far to the west and too far in the past. Far from being a myth the story was a precise account of the volcanic disintegration of an island in the Minoan empire.

The man who delivered Egypt from Persian rule and implanted Greek culture was a pupil of Aristotle, who in turn had studied with Plato. A Macedonian from the Greek fringe, Alexander came to Egypt with an open-hearted readiness to endorse its values. His attitude to foreign cultures was uncharacteristic of most Greeks, who used the term 'barbarian' to signify what was not their own. Nothing in his career pleased Alexander more than the recognition by the oracle in the Siwa oasis that he, the reputed son of Philip, was in fact the son of Ammon.

For the first time in Egypt's long history a foreign force was to affect Egypt deeply and for a very long time. Having visited Memphis, Alexander decided to found a new capital on a fishermen's island off the delta, separated from Egypt by Lake Mariut. From this city of Alexandria a Hellenizing influnce was to permeate the adjacent delta, the Nile valley, and the attached oasis of Fayum. One of Alexander's generals, Ptolemaus, inherited Egypt when Alexander died near the original Babylon in Mesopotamia; Ptolemaus bequeathed it as a kingdom to more than a dozen generations of descendants. Ptolemaic Alexandria was a city where Europe, Africa, and Asia met. The Ptolemaic legacy—in particular to the West—was opulent; to the Egyptians it was gained at the price of colonial rule. It was a form of colonial rule whose tolerance made it the more difficult to resist. No instance of modern colonialism affords a parallel. Post-Renaissance empires, varied as they have been, have manifested, each in its own form, the Hebraic principle: Thou shalt have no other gods but Me (the 'Me' being an astonishing spectrum of intolerances). The Greeks, imitating Alexander, were to intermarry with the subject races. They had no attachment to one faith. On the contrary they sought for correlations between the occupants of their own Olympus and the gods of foreigners.

To picture an equivalent of the Greek symbiosis with Egypt one would have to imagine an Anglo-Saxon occupation of India lasting not two centuries but ten and marked, from the beginning, by a passionate and continuous absorption of Hindu rituals. Lords Curzon and Reading and ten generations of successors would have dressed themselves in the panoply of rajahs, while English sovereigns would have reigned as avatars of Indian gods from Balmorals rebuilt to resemble the temples of Madura. Their pallid corpses would have been burned on Ganges pyres or digested by vultures in the towers of silence.

The dynasty of Ptolemaus, and after its extinction, its Roman inheritors, played this role in Egypt. The Ptolemies shook off the taboos of their native land, starting with incest, the most horrendous sin of classical Hellas. Osiris had married his sister Isis; many pharaohs, inheriting through the female line, had done the same thing. The Ptolemies piously begot children by their sisters; the last effective monarch of the race, Cleopatra, was the comely result of this procedure. They patronized the gods of their adopted land. Sculpted as pharaohs, they rebuilt derelict temples and scrupulously maintained the timeworn rites. To bind the Greek colonists with the Egyptian majority, a new god, Serapis, was consciously created. (He had a considerable success outside as well as inside Egypt.) Serapis was a fusion of two Pharaonic gods: Osiris, the lord of the afterworld, and Apis, the divine bull; these two deities had more popular resonance than the intellectual of Memphis, Ptah, or Ammon, originally an Ethiopic god. In appearance Serapis was a riverine ancient in the Greek manner: bearded, he supported on his tangled locks a basket of mysteries.

The Greek appetite for mysteries was insatiable. Perhaps because they were so rational themselves, the Greeks eagerly sought what refuted logic. They had practiced mysteries at home in a dull Athenian suburb. In Egypt with its weird animal gods, its nocturnal rites, its cryptic tongue, its ambiguous texts, they had stumbled on a fascinating vein. They would mine its most jaded seams. In a second-century necropolis at Alexandria—an underground Forest Lawn of the pagan world—they stacked their loved ones amidst a fusion of Greek and Egyptian modes: Anubis, the jackal-faced undertaker god, is dressed in Greek costume complete with military boots, while a European dignitary with the curly hair of a Praxiteles stands in the rigid Pharaonic pose.

In return for these mystic borrowings the Greeks brought gifts of their own: a language more supple than any other and a naturalistic style of art which would leave its impress in Egypt, as it would farther east, in Buddhist lands.

Yet linguistic subtleties and the philosophical ideas they made possible did little for the native Egyptians, for the people we may imagine living in Babylon-in-Egypt as well as the now declining cities of Memphis and Heliopolis. Greek naturalism was not only to overthrow the priestly art of Egypt (from which the art of archaic Greece had distantly derived) but to destroy the credibility of the symbols which this art purveyed. Despite their eager patronage of the mysterious, the Greeks themselves could not quite believe, however hard they tried. They loved philosophic argument more than magic. In the tenebrous vaults of Thebes someone who signs himself 'Nicagoras of Athens' has scrawled the following prayer:

Be gracious to me here also, Plato.

Against their will, the Greeks had killed the mysteries they wished to serve. Plato was more potent as a god than Horus (both hawkshaped solar god and son of Isis), in whose honor the Ptolemies had rebuilt the Edfu temple. For the Egyptians Plato was no substitute for the gods in whom they increasingly disbelieved.

There was no real fusion between the mind of Alexandria and the mind of Babylon-in-Egypt. The Greeks were inquisitive, experimental, articulate; the Egyptians were patient, conservative, secretive. The Greeks believed in speculation and reason, the Egyptians in magic which could raise them children or crops, or bring curses on a neighbor.

Babylon-in-Egypt was a town where Egyptians lived in surly amity beside their masters. These masters were preponderantly Greek even when, from the death of Cleopatra to the founding of

Constantinople, Egypt was a part of an empire ruled from Rome. Latin never became the lingua franca of the eastern portions of the empire, whose culture was consistently Hellenistic. The Roman contribution to Egyptian history was almost nil, though Roman methods of building, transmitted to the Byzantines, strengthened the walls and buttresses of Babylon. Those emperors who took an interest in Egyptian culture—such as Hadrian, who founded the city of Antinoöpolis on the Nileside site of his favorite's suicide—were themselves completely Hellenized. Others merely regarded the delta as a cornucopia for the imperial populace.

Alexandria was the city where the Hellenic mind fused not with the Egyptian, but with the Hebrew. The relation between the Greeks and the Jews was ultimately one of violent antagonism. The majority of pious Jews would always see in the Hellenic tradition a compound of idolatry and human self-worship repellent to Israel. But under the Ptolemies these very opposed ways of looking at the world interacted creatively, if briefly.[1] Thanks to Ptolemaic encouragement the Hebrew scriptures were translated into Greek; a Jewish temple at Leontopolis in the delta was founded under the same kindly rule. A double process was at work. The Jews of Alexandria (more broad-minded than those in Palestine) began to recognize that the terms of Greek philosophy could deepen their understanding of their ancestral faith. The Greeks, always thirsty for a new idea, toyed with identifying the Almighty of scripture with the Platonic absolute from whom lower forms had all evolved. The medium between the transcendent and the near was the Logos, or creative Word.

The incarnate Logos came first not to coastal Alexandria with its sumptuous palaces, its spectacular Serapeum and munificent library, but to the huddled inland town of Babylon-in-Egypt. The Logos, in appearance an infant refugee, passed the customs post at the village of Qantara to enter an Egypt which had become the private estate of Augustus Caesar, Cleopatra's vanquisher. The prefect of the province was Gaius Turranius. With the child traveled his mother, his putative father, and the midwife Salome. They went first to Bilbeis, a delta town not far from the place where the ancient Hebrews had toiled in bondage. On their way to Babylon they passed the colonnades and porticoes of Ptolemaic Heliopolis. As the donkeys of the Holy

Family trotted into the decaying city the statues of the pagan gods (recognizing that truth had come) fell crashing to the ground. The Fountain of the Sun, which gave the city its name, delighted the Virgin, many of whose later apparitions, as at Walsingham and Lourdes, were to be concerned with wells and springs. Her sojourn in Heliopolis (on the site of the modern suburb of Mattariya) has made the spring of fresh water and its surrounding trees a place of pilgrimage throughout the centuries. Piloti, a medieval traveler, describes what has hardly changed today:

> Near Cairo, going three miles towards Jerusalem, is a garden which is called Mattaria, where is a well worked in white marble which seems as though it had been made today. It is full of sweet water in which Our Lady washed the clothes of Our Lord Jesus Christ.

The Egyptian exile of the Holy Family has been denied by critics. Some argue that the story is a pious fiction designed to fulfill the scriptural prophecy "Out of Egypt have I called my son."[2] Similar criticisms were long leveled at Homer's description of windy Troy or Herodotus' account of a canal across the isthmus of Corinth. Archaeology confirms more often than it refutes such persistent traditions. There can, however, be no archaeological evidence for this journey by humble people. Yet we know enough of the classical world to recognize that the ancients traveled widely. Egypt, with its numerous Jewish colonies, was a most convenient place of refuge. The unanimous tradition of centuries associates Jesus and his mother with numerous places in Egypt, though never with Alexandria. In old Cairo a church contains a crypt that has long been revered as the home of the refugees.

"The fourth church we entered," wrote a traveler in the fourteenth century, as we might write today, "is called St. Mary of the Cave. It is where Our Lady lived with her son when she fled from Syria with Joseph and when they took refuge in Egypt out of obedience to the warning Joseph received in Bethlehem that Herod was looking for Jesus to kill him. They stayed there seven years. It is an underground place. You go down by a staircase of nine steps."

There is no reason to suppose that the Holy Family had a penchant for crypts. The deposit of centuries has laid layer upon layer. What was ground level in the first century is many steps below ground level now. If any place is awe-filled this place is.

From their base in Babylon—only a short walk from an ancient synagogue—the Holy Family are reputed to have traveled upriver as far as the site of Deir al-Muharraq, a later monastery. As traveler's checks Saint Joseph used the gold, myrrh, and frankincense brought by the Wise Men. Then Herod died and the Holy Family returned to Palestine—Christ to study the scriptures which he would fulfill in Jerusalem in Easter week.

Egypt took to the new religion with a fervor in tune with its millennial religious zeal. According to the Acts of the Apostles, Egyptians were present in Jerusalem on the day of Pentecost. These were either Egyptian Jews or Greek converts to the new syncretic doctrines of Philo of Alexandria. They would have returned to Egypt inflamed with the new faith. St. Mark is traditionally regarded as the first bishop of Alexandria, but the conception of 'bishop' needs scrubbing to see him right. He was more like the cell leader of a modern seditious movement. A verse at the end of St. Peter's first epistle has been taken by some commentators to refer to a cell already existing in Babylon; the same verse includes a reference to St. Mark.[3]

Alexandria with a Hellenistic upper class and Babylon with an Egyptian lower class, accepted Christ in two distinct and separate ways.

The Greeks accepted the Word as the intellectual solution to a world of doubt. (Those Greeks who rejected him did so in favor of an etherealized philosophy refurbished to rival the moral purity of the new faith.) The Greeks were active in the wrangles that, over a few centuries, defined Christian doctrine. The creeds that remain the formal statement of Christian belief are the achievement of men who thought in Greek and lived in Egypt.

The Egyptians, whether fellahin or artisans, accepted Christ as an incarnate god showing a way to escape from sin. (Those Egyptians who rejected him did so in favor of magic.) Christ completed the Egyptian pattern of metaphysical development as much as he completed the patterns of the Greeks and the Jews.

From the beginning the Egyptians had been obsessed with the afterlife. The Pharaonic edifices which survive were nearly all concerned with death. The pyramids, far from being works of self-glory like the statues of Ramses II, were the chief statement of this obsession. The thousands who had labored to build them believed that in creating ladders to heaven for their god–kings, they were preparing ladders for themselves. They were present in their king as the congregation of a Catholic church are present in their priest.

With the development of Pharaonic civilization, ideas about the afterlife developed. Individuals began to hope for personal salvation, or survival. Important officials began to build their own houses for eternity; it was felt that only those who could afford embalming and the right mortuary ceremonies would live again. The poor were thus excluded, except as servants, from the cheerful Nilotic paradise portrayed on the walls of the rich men's tombs.

Toward the end of the Pharaonic period the god Osiris became not merely a magical guardian of the afterworld but a moral judge. To be properly embalmed, to have the correct spells written around your corpse, was not enough. You had also to make the 'negative confession'—that you had not committed the major sins—to the dark powers of death.

Christ's promise that the sins of believers would be forgiven opened paradise to all. But the gloom of centuries still haunted the Egyptians. Salvation could not be easy. They looked in the new sacred texts and found proofs that they were right. Christ's offer of salvation was on severe moral terms. There had to be a rejection of the old, a rebirth of the new. The Egyptian Christians (who are called Copts[4]) were less tolerant of their pagan past than were the Greeks. While some Greek Christians continued to find merits in Plato, the Copts turned on their ancient religion with vengeful fury. History affords no parallel of a nation so radically rejecting its past. Descendants of the soldiers of Pharaoh emotionally identified themselves with the Children of Israel who had fled from their ancestors' power. They took biblical names; they fashioned a new, earthy art. Sometimes, as an afterthought, an ancient symbol would survive: the ankh of Akhnaton ☥ would be used as though it were a cross. But the spirit of Coptic art was totally removed from the tired art of the later pharaohs. It was fresh, rustic, working-class. Realistic, at times humorous, it reflected plebeian or agricultural concerns. Both finicky and crude, it inspired attractive textiles, delicate carvings, and some moving religious art. The influence of Greece—more acceptable now that the Greeks were Christians too—was stronger than the influence of Pharaonic Egypt. The demotic alphabet of the pharaohs was exchanged for an alphabet modeled on Greek; hundreds of Greek words were borrowed to express truths now shared by all men, not held as arcane secrets by a few.

The Copts contributed more to the disciplines than to the metaphysics of Christian life. Monasticism, their greatest contribution, was the response of Egyptian literalism to the gospel summons to perfection. St. Antony was an Upper Egyptian Copt who heard the command "If you would be perfect, sell all you have and give to the poor," and acted on it. He sold what he had, put his sister in a hostel for secluded women, and started a movement of withdrawal which in a short time crowded the Nile valley and its surrounding deserts with clusters of hermits' cells or barracklike monasteries where converted fellahin toiled and prayed under the stern lash of a spiritual praetorian in God. (A Coptic monastery still stands at the southern boundary of Cairo, on the banks of the Nile. It marks the spot where the Holy Family supposedly embarked on a felucca for Upper Egypt.)

In theory the Greeks and the Copts were brothers in Christ. In practice the Greeks gathered the taxes and ruled while the Copts produced the food and were taxed. Despite the claim of Constantinople to be a new, baptized Rome (it was inaugurated as such in AD 330), it remained a city where politicians practiced their fraudulent arts. The coming of the Gospel did not mean that there were no more prisons, no more extortions, no more judicial deaths. The Christianization of the empire by Constantine marked a watershed of disillusion for many Christians. The new dawn of grace was depressingly like the old evening of sin. It soon accentuated the rift between Greeks and Copts in Egypt. St. Antony, when over a hundred, had journeyed on foot from his Red Sea monastery of Alexandria, there to support Athanasius in his great contest with Arius over the nature of Christ. While Arius argued that "there had been a time when the son was not," Antony agreed with Athanasius that both Son and Father were one, with the Spirit, co-eternal persons of one God. But after the fourth century relations between Greek and Copt were increasingly strained.

The upper-class view of the Copts is shown by Ammianus, the last important classical historian, a fourth-century Greek from Antioch. A military man, he knew all the eastern empire well. "The Egyptian is ashamed if he cannot show his lean, brown body marked with welts upon welts received for his refusal to pay taxes. No physical torture has yet been discovered"—it sounds as though the Greeks needed modern help—"to make a hardened Egyptian robber acknowledge his name."

The Copts expressed their alienation from their Greek masters by exaggerating slight differences in metaphysical terms until a schism formed two mutually hostile communions: the Monophysite Coptic church headed by its own patriarch in Alexandria and the Byzantine (or Malikite) church with its patriarch in Constantinople.

By the early seventh century the Copts not only hated Byzantium but despised it, too. The emperor Heraklius was determined to force a new compromise variant of Christianity on all his subjects. At the same time he was unable to protect the Holy Places. In AD 619, for the second time since the conversion of Constantine, Jerusalem was occupied by those to whom Jesus was not a sacred person. Such occupations seemed destined to presage disasters to the occupiers. The first had been the emperor Julian. The Apostate had contemplated building a pagan temple on Mount Moriah and importing fanatical Jews to safeguard the city against a Christian return. Julian's death in battle against Persia led to the final defeat of the paganism he had loved. Now the king of Persia had occupied Jerusalem and carried off the Holy Cross. To the Copts Jerusalem, then as now, was the center of devotion. Its loss lowered Byzantine prestige as never before.

The Persian occupation of the Holy City coincided with unnoticed developments in backward Arabia. In 622 an Arabian called Muhammad abandoned Mecca, the holy city of pagan Arabia, in order to preach his monotheistic faith in greater freedom. The city to which he migrated was, as Medina, to be the capital of a suddenly expanding state; the year of his migration was to be the start of an era. The year before Muhammad died in AD 632, Heraklius managed to drive the Zoroastrian Persians back into their mountains. His triumph was short-lived. Within a few years the armed missionaries of Islam burst from an Arabia newly united in the faith of Muhammad. The Persian empire was to be destroyed, the Byzantine empire to be reduced by half.

The Arabians were by no means strangers to Egypt. The citizens of Babylon were used to the arrival of caravans bringing the spices of the south to the markets outside their walls. The Arabians also knew Egypt well. The man who was to conquer it for Islam—Amr ibn al-As—had himself visited Egypt, before his conversion, when he had been in charge of a commercial caravan.

But in AD 641 the Arabians arrived in greater numbers than before, and in a different spirit. The great gates of Babylon were closed as what looked like an armed camp sprang up outside the walls. This time the Arabians had come not as traders but as preachers. Their creed, the stronger for being short, rang out at the times of prayer: "No deity but God; Muhammad is the Prophet of God." The challenge brought by the Muslim leaders was equally simple: The people inside Babylon could submit to the doctrines revealed in the Koran (this 'submission' is the primary meaning of Islam) or they could remain Christians (the Koran recognized them as well as Jews as 'people of the Book') but pay a poll tax. The tax was significantly lower than the one they were already paying to their Greek overlords; men of religion were exempt from the tax altogether.

The tensions discussed in this chapter must have been in the minds of the men now besieged behind the stout Roman walls of Babylon. As they peeped over the parapets at the Bedouin camp on the empty plain to the north, as they heard the Call to Prayer, as they saw the massed soldiers prostrating themselves like one vast creature toward Mecca, they must have argued among themselves: Were these enemies, to be resisted in the name of Christian unity? Or were they saviors from a Christian disunity which had brought them misery?

The issue was not decided in one night. The Arabians had easily overrun the imperial forces at Heliopolis but it took them a seven-month siege before Babylon surrendered. Brilliant practitioners of desert warfare, the Arabians had yet to master the two techniques of fighting at sea and of investing fortified cities. During the protracted siege there were frequent probes from each side as to the intentions of the other.

The chroniclers have preserved an account of what the Egyptians found when they sent one embassy to the camp of Amr. "We found," they told the Byzantine governor, "a people who love death better than life, and set humility above pride; who have no desire or enjoyment in this world, who sit in the dust and eat upon their knees, but frequently and thoroughly wash, and humble themselves in prayer; a people in whom the stronger can scarce be distinguished from the weaker, or the master from the slave."

To many Copts these democratic Muslims must have seemed attractive; or if not attractive, then useful counterweights to the immemorial tyranny of Rome, whether old or new. (To later Muslims the description of their forebears just quoted must have made as ironic reading as early Christian history made to victims of Byzantine cruelty and court intrigue.)

In April 641, with incalculable results for the Copts and the world, the City of Babylon opened its gates to the representative of the caliph in Medina. By the end of the summer the imperial capital of Alexandria had also surrendered and Egypt had become a province of Islam.

4

Fustat
City of the Tent

Aмr was not a free agent in Egypt. He held his governorship on authority from Omar, the second successor (or caliph) of the Prophet. Amr himself had been captivated by an Alexandria whose Pharos still stood and whose two marbled streets still intersected at Alexander's tomb. In a report to Omar he had let himself go: it was, he wrote, a city with "4,000 palaces, 4,000 baths, 12,000 dealers in fresh oil, 12,000 gardeners, 40,000 Jews who pay tribute, 400 theaters or places of amusement." He did not mention (or burn) the great library; civil dissension and Christian dislike of pagan authors had long since scattered its 700,000 volumes. He cannot fail to have noticed the contrast between Cairo's torrid summer and the fresh breezes of the seaside town.

To Amr's enthusiastic dispatch, and his suggestion that Alexandria should be the capital of Muslim Egypt, the caliph returned a chilly answer.

"In that case," Omar asked, "will there be water between me and the Muslim army?"

Amr had to admit there would be. Alexandria was a long narrow city, running east and west, cut off from Egypt by Lake Mariut but linked to the western branch of the Nile by a canal. At the time of the Nile floods (which Amr had seen for himself) the delta became a lake and the city was isolated from the interior.

Land communications with Arabia would be entirely cut. The sea which washed Alexandria on its northern side was also perilous to the Arabs, who at this time had no fleet. If the Byzantines were to counterattack, this would be the way they would come. (They did so a few years later when Amr was dismissed from his governorship by Omar's successor, Uthman; only the restoration of the respected Amr led to the recapture of the city for Islam.)

Amr, therefore, returned to Babylon-in-Egypt with the command to choose a new site in the vicinity of Memphis. But it would have to be on the east bank, the side nearer to Arabia. The building of a new capital was part of Omar's policy in all but one of the occupied territories. In Syria (which was already heavily impregnated with Arabian influences) the Muslims had taken over Damascus, at first sharing its great church with the Christians. In countries remoter from Arabian influence Omar planned to create separate barrack towns from which to administer provinces not converted to Islam but paying instead the poll tax provided for in all Muslim treaties. He did not wish his ardent soldiers to grow soft or to acquire land and settle down. The new Egyptian city would be similar in structure to Kufa and Basra in Iraq, or Kairouan in Tunisia.

As usual a picturesque tale accounts for the choice Amr made of a new site. He had left his military tent (in Arabic *fustat*) standing just to the north of Babylon, close to the Nile, when he had gone north to besiege Alexandria. On his return it was still standing; in a fold in its goat-hair hangings a dove had made its nest. Amr declared the site sacred and declared that the bird was to be left undisturbed. When her brood was raised he founded his mosque on this site and round it grew Misr-al-Fustat, City of the Tent.

Such a gentle gesture is not inconceivable. Amr was an impassioned Muslim and Muslims at this time glowed with the charisma of their revolutionary faith.

But Amr was also an astute general and a much traveled man. It was he who suggested the conquest of Egypt to Omar, on the basis of his own journeys to the country before the coming of Islam. He recognized the value of this particular site for his administrative capital. The area where he had encamped was on its west side defended (and watered) by the Nile; on the south there were the existing fortifications of Babylon-in-Egypt; to the north and east he could supplement the existing canal with a defensive ditch. (The Byzantine term for such a military ditch was *fossaton*—from a military viewpoint a more likely derivation for the name Fustat.) Once properly defended, this site would be an ideal position from which to control the country and to communicate with the Arabian headquarters of Islam. Caravan routes led east from Babylon to the Gulf of Suez; there they divided, one route going north to Palestine and Syria, the other south to western Arabia. The partly choked canal—known as the Amnis Traianus in Roman times, because of Trajan's efforts in keeping it clear—could easily be repaired. This would enable Egyptian agricultural surplus to be shipped home to the needy Arabian towns. The site was also bare. Except for a few scattered churches and convents, it consisted of fields and wasteland. It was also large. Size was important for Amr's purpose. He not only needed a barrack town, he needed a large barrack town in which the various Arabian tribes could be given separate regions; this was the only way to prevent those who had been feuding enemies before Islam from becoming enemies again.

The focus of the new city was its mosque.

Compared with modern notions of what a mosque should be— these notions being formed from awareness of an architectural development of more than thirteen centuries—it was a primitive affair. It reflected, indeed, the simplicity of the country from which Amr came. "It would appear that the pre-Islamic Arabs had but the crudest notions of building, that their principal sanctuary before 608 was nothing more than four walls the height of a man enclosing the sacred well Zemzem, and that in the early days of Islam they brought nothing architectural to the conquered countries beyond what would serve their simple ritual requirements."[1] Muhammad's own headquarters in Medina had consisted, according to an eyewitness, of "four houses of mud brick, with apartments partitioned off by palm branches plastered with mud, and five houses made of palm branches plastered with mud and not divided into rooms. Over the doors were curtains of black haircloth. Each curtain measured three by three cubits. One could touch the roof with the hand."

The building was put up during the winter of 640–641. It consisted of a rectangular room measuring about ninety-five by fifty-six feet. Its walls were of rough mud brick; palm-bole pillars probably supported a ceiling of palm planks, themselves supporting a roof made of palm leaves and daub. There was no courtyard, no minaret, no niche pointing the direction for prayer and no decorations. The floor was strewn with pebbles. It had two doors on each side except the side facing Mecca.

Amr himself led his soldiers in prayer and delivered a sermon:

> The Nile floods have risen. The grazing will be good. There is milk for the lambs and kids. Go out with God's blessing and enjoy the land, its milk, its flocks and its herds, and take good care of your neighbors, the Copts, for the Prophet of God himself gave orders for us so to do.

The reference to the Copts as neighbors was not metaphorical. Fustat's flimsy buildings stretched in a great arc from the fortress and churches of Babylon up toward the Mokattam hills. Although the military town was deliberately kept distinct from the Coptic city, this did not prevent the Muslims from establishing friendly relations with its citizens. Markets sprang up between the tented town and Babylon. The Muslims depended on the local people for food as well as for clerical assistance in running the country. For more than a generation the administration was to be conducted in Coptic or Greek.

As the two groups tended to coalesce, so some Copts were converted to Islam. The fervent Muslim missionaries argued that in accepting Muhammad as God's Prophet the Copt would be accepting the Comforter promised by Christ himself. The traditional teaching of the Church was that the Comforter had already come, in the person of the Holy Ghost, the spirit that would lead men into truth. Some Copts may have doubted whether the wrangling disputes from which they had suffered could be the result of divine guidance. It was tempting to recognize the Comforter in a man recently alive, rather than in a spirit symbolized by a bird. The Koran confirmed, rather than refuted, much that the Copts believed and practiced. The day-long fasting prescribed for Ramadan resembled the penitential fasts of these Egyptian Christians. The Koran paid high honor to both Jesus and his mother, the latter the only woman to be mentioned by name in the new holy book.

There were other than theological arguments for accepting the new faith. In Muslim theory, anyone who recited the Islamic creed before witnesses became *ipso facto* a member of the Islamic nation. This nation, rapidly spreading throughout the world, enjoyed privileges denied to the tolerated but not entirely equal members of older monotheistic religions. By becoming a Muslim the convert would become, in theory at least, the equal of the Arabian rulers.

If practical motives tempted Copts to conversion, so opposite practical motives tempted Muslims to forget their basic principles. The interests of the Islamic state warred with its doctrines. While its preachers urged all men to become Muslims, those running its exchequer preferred that Christians should remain what they were and pay the poll tax.

As the normal routine of politics took over from the first idealistic rush, as the needs of an expanding empire became more pressing, as the rulers of this empire tended to become the practical and the ambitious, not the pious and the austere, so the governors of Egypt required more money and more food—precisely the requirements of the Byzantine governors before them. For at least a century distinction was made between Arabian and non-Arabian Muslims, the latter suffering disabilities, the former constituting an effective elite.

For the Christians who remained faithful to their faith one immediate result of the Islamic conquest was the sudden efflorescence of a Coptic literature (admittedly restricted to works of a sacred nature) which began after the collapse of Byzantine power. Coptic artists in stone, wood, ivory, and textiles (already renowned under the Byzantines) found eager employers in the Muslim rulers, who increasingly wished to embellish their mosques and palaces. Coptic workmen found outlets outside Egypt. All over the Near East the new rulers were busy building.

In Fustat the mosque of Amr soon proved too small. Within a generation the caliph Muawiya, reigning from Damascus, ordered the ninth governor of Egypt to enlarge it. What Amr had built was pulled down and a larger enclosure was made; this time its walls were covered with plaster, whereas rush matting took the place of pebbles on the floor. An open court was added to the northwest. At each corner of the enlarged mosque rudimentary minarets were recorded as having been built; these were either wooden platforms or short towers. The second mosque dated from 673.

Fustat grew fast as Islam became rooted in Egypt. In another generation the mosque needed to be enlarged once more. This third construction was made between 710 and 712. This time the mosque was given a prayer niche (or *mihrab*), inspired by the curved recesses in Coptic churches. Just a century later the mosque was again enlarged, this time being doubled in size. It now had thirteen doors. Instead of the primitive pillars of date boles, 378 columns supported those parts of the mosque which provided shade. The columns were not the work of contemporary stonemasons. They were purloined from the temples of Memphis, or from churches in disuse.

Again and again this first mosque of Cairo was to be rebuilt. After periodic lapses into disrepair it would be restored by some energetic ruler who felt the pull of its prestige. Enlarged and changed though it has been, the spirit of early Islam has stubbornly refused to be banished in any of its rebuildings. The large, ill-patronized mosque of the twentieth century, though in no concrete sense what it was when Amr built it, is in direct descent from the humble room in which the first Egyptian Muslims said their prayers, and in which the Copts were first invited to join the faith.

Outside the walls of this great mosque the two communities of Egypt, in the centuries after Amr, were to follow divergent paths. The Muslims, slowly expanding to their present ninety per cent, were to be the dominant community, though themselves dominated by rulers from outside Egypt. Copts in their dark churches would continue offering prayers to Jesus and his mother as well as to the Father and Holy Spirit. Young men in each generation would forsake the world and become monks. But the Copts, under the Byzantines a suppressed majority, were to become, under the Muslims, a suppressed minority. The tolerance of Amr was at times to be denied them. These bad times depended on the whims of fanatical interpreters of the Islamic law; or they were the result of political tension between Islam and Christendom. When, for example, the Crusaders invaded Palestine, the chief victims were the eastern Christians.

The Coptic neighbor was suspected as a secret ally of the bully with the cross.

It is a tribute to the spiritual wisdom of Egyptian Islam—a spirit that still seems to haunt the structure of Amr's much changed mosque—that despite these tensions Christianity was never eradicated from Egypt as it has been from the rest of Muslim North Africa. The Coptic Easter has become the national spring holiday of *sham al-nesseem*— literally 'smelling the breeze'—shared by Egyptians of all faiths. It is a tribute to the tenacity of the Copts that even now a daily liturgy embodying passages in the language of the pharaohs is recited all over Egypt. There are probably as many Easter communicants in Egypt as Catholic communicants in New York.

5

Ibn Tulun
First Independent Ruler of Egypt
Since Cleopatra

For TWO HUNDRED YEARS Egypt was ruled as a governorate of the Muslim caliphate. As this religious empire evolved, Egypt's affairs were controlled successively from Medina in Arabia, Damascus in Syria, and Baghdad in Iraq. As part of this early Islamic empire Egypt experienced the same metaphysical winds as Iraq, Persia and Spain.

One bitter eastern wind was a sense of disillusion not dissimilar to that which had played an important role in 'opening' (the Arabic metaphor for conquest) Egypt for Islam. The seventh-century Copts had resented an alien Byzantine government whose acts belied the Christian principles which it professed. By the ninth century a similar mood had built up toward a caliphate which had now become not the unknown rebel but the known authority.

In Islam political power proved as agonizing a trap as in Christendom. In a sense Christians were disillusioned less easily, not having been prepared for a kingdom of justice upon earth. In the first three centuries the Church had been an underground movement in the Roman empire. This buried time had served to impose on the Christian mind a bifocal vision which it was seldom to lose, a vision made easy for Christians by their master's differentiation between what belonged to Caesar and what belonged to God. Even when Caesar became a

Christian emperor, an always articulate and often rebellious hierarchy maintained the dual vision. This distinction between secular and sacred (destined to sharpen in a Latin Europe split between Holy Roman Emperor and Pope) was something Christianity gained from its birth in a despised province of the Roman empire.

Islam had experienced an apparently easier birth in its wild Arabian cradle. Though persecuted by the upper-class polytheists of Mecca, Muhammad had managed to establish a state obedient to himself in the northern city of Medina. It was as though Christ, by some miraculous *coup d'état,* had seized and exercised the powers of the Sanhedrin and Pontius Pilate. Muhammad in the last ten years of his life was no mere visionary seer but the day-to-day ruler of a state having powers of life and death over all its members. This Islamic government made no distinction between the sacred and the secular. For instance, the paying of *zakat,* the alms commanded by the Koran, was a civic duty. It could be enforced by the law. A failure to fast in Ramadan could be punished by a governmental flogging. When Muhammad died in 632 his role of Prophet died with him; he bequeathed his other roles to his elderly friend and father-in-law, the pious Abu Bakr.

As caliph (that is, successor) Abu Bakr carried on the work of Muhammad. This was not simply to preach and practice a religion; it was to offer membership in a dynamic new community, a church lacking priests and sacraments but possessing an army and a collective missionary aim. Abut Bakr's greatest achievement in a two-year reign was his reimposition of Islam on a tribal Arabia which at first apostasized (thinking the bond between the tribes and Muhammad merely temporary) on the Prophet's death. The second caliph, Omar, propelled the missionary soldiers of this re-Islamized Arabia into Iraq, Syria, and Egypt.

Thus very early in its apostolic period Islam was forced to confront, and to try to solve, the problems of power. (These had remained theoretical for Christians until Constantine's conversion.) Within a very short time the apostolic charisma was stained with blood. Abu Bakr died in his bed; not so his three successors. The determined and scrupulous Omar was stabbed while at prayer in the Medina mosque; the dying caliph expressed himself happy that since the assassin was a Persian non-Muslim, he would go, as a martyr, straight to heaven. But the third caliph, the aristocratic Uthman, was murdered by fellow Muslims; they spilled his octogenarian blood over the Koran whose text he had codified. Egypt was involved with the motives of his murderers. The rather weak Uthman was accused of having replaced Amr with a time-serving relative who had adopted Islam only for the opportunities it offered for personal gain.

The fourth caliph, Ali, had the most tragic fate of all. No one had been closer to the Prophet. Ali's father, Abu Taleb, had brought up Muhammad in his own house, since Abdulla, Muhammad's father, had died before his birth and Amina, his mother, when he was a child. Ali was one of the first three male Muslims (the first Muslim of all had been Khadija, Muhammad's wife) and was married to Fatima, Muhammad's daughter by Khadija. Fatima bore him two sons, Hassan and Hussein.

Ali embodied to an outstanding degree the Arabian ideals of what a man should be: eloquent, open-handed, and brave. Yet his claim to the caliphate had been overlooked by the rough consensus of the Muslim community which elected the first three caliphs. Perhaps the Muslims sensed Ali's unfitness for the role of politician. When in 656 Ali was at last elected, those who had hoped that an intimate relative of the Prophet could reknit the fabric of Islam were to be disappointed.

Tragically, Ali owed his election to the murder of Uthman and Uthman belonged to the most powerful single family in Mecca, the Omayyads. This family, though kin to Muhammad, had persecuted Islam when it was struggling to birth and joined it when its cause was triumphant and profitable. Uthman had promoted Omayyads during his caliphate, tilting the balance from the revolutionary toward the conservative. His most brilliant relative was Muawiya, a politician in every fiber, whom he created governor of Damascus. On Uthman's death, Muawiya displayed his uncle's bloodstained robe in the mosque at Damascus and demanded vengeance. He would not recognize Ali as caliph until Ali had punished the murderers of Uthman; if Ali failed, then, Muawiya implied, he must be their accomplice.

Against the shrewd political skills of Muawiya and his ability to call on the support of men like Amr, Ali could at first count on the pious, the poor, and the non-Arabian converts, in particular the Persians. He was to lose much of this support when after the battle between his army and the Syrian army of his rival he submitted his claims to arbitration. Muawiya's army had been led by Amr who, facing apparent defeat, thought of a brilliant ruse: his soldiers hoisted copies of the Koran on their lances and called for the arbitrament of God.

Some of Ali's most fervent supporters—those who saw Islam as a community of the saved, not a political organism—attacked him for submitting something as sacred as the imamate (the headship of Islam) to human election. One group of such people planned to solve the problems of divided Islam by arranging three assassinations on one day: of Amr in Egypt, of Muawiya in Damascus, and of Ali in Kufa, his barrack city in Iraq. Only the assassination of Ali succeeded. Power was now firmly in the hands of Muawiya who moved the capital of Islam to Damascus. He founded a hereditary dynasty which in a century was to conquer a vast empire stretching from Spain in the west to Central Asia in the east. During this century Egypt was ruled from Damascus.

But behind the facade of Islamic triumph there was a fundamental split in the minds of Muslims. Many saw in the Omayyads worldly opportunists who simply used Islam to cement a kingdom hardly better than other kingdoms. The fate of Ali's descendants increased resentment. While Hassan renounced his claims to the caliphate in return for a princely stipend and a life of debauchery, Hussein waited for the death of Muawiya to lead an insurrection against Muawiya's son Yezid. Hussein and most of his family, lured to Iraq by misleading promises to support, were massacred after a long ordeal outside the town of Kerbela.

The tragic fate of the Prophet's nearest descendant stirred the imagination of Muslims. Ali had been killed on his way to prayer and the grandchild whom Muhammad had dandled on his knee had been decapitated by brother Muslims. As the bright hopes of early Islam were disappointed, as the dream of a new society became simply a new oppression, many Muslims saw in the treatment of Ali's family a basic sin which would continue to smear Islam until a new imam, or infallible guide, was accepted from his descendants. This Shia, or party, of Ali particularly attracted Persian Muslims who found that, despite their conversion, they were not treated as the equals of Arabians. The Shia formed a political movement embodying nostalgia for a lost charisma and the dream of a messianic age. Its basic tenet was that God would not leave his people without a guide. In every age a descendant of Ali would constitute a divinely inspired imam; when the visible descendants of Ali's line ran out, pious fancy produced the attractive notion of a 'hidden imam,' a Messiah biding his time.

The Shia were to play an important role in molding the climate of opinion in which the Omayyad dynasty was destroyed in AD 750. Emissaries of another Meccan branch of the Prophet's wide-ranging clan, the descendants of his uncle Abbas, used the sympathies of the Shia as well as Persian nationalist resentment at Arabian supremacy to undermine Omayyad control.

The result of widespread disillusion with the Omayyad oligarchy was a military revolt in Khorasan led by Abu Muslim, a Persian soldier of genius. The last Omayyad caliph, Marwan, escaped to Egypt. After setting fire to Fustat and the wooden bridge which linked it to Roda Island, he took refuge on the west bank. But the Persian soldiers under an Abbasid general discovered his hiding place and paraded his lopped-off head round the ruined town before sending it back to army headquarters in Iraq. Marwan's fate was shared by nearly all his family. Ninety of his relatives, promised an amnesty by an uncle of the new Abbasid caliph, were invited to a banquet and treacherously slaughtered. The corpses were covered with leather mats and the planned banquet enjoyed on top of them. One Omayyad managed to reach Muslim Spain and there start an independent dynasty.

Though Islam was no longer coterminous with the caliphate, Egypt was now ruled by a caliph living in Iraq.

The first Abbasid caliph, al-Saffah ('the Slaughterer'), sent a governor to Egypt with instructions to rebuild the capital, but not on the site of Fustat, which was associated with the Omayyads. Known as Medinat al-Askar, or City of Cantonments, this new capital lay to the north of Amr's town. Its chief building was a large congregational mosque designed to rival Amr's. Each great Islamic city required one large mosque where all the male faithful could gather at noon on Friday to pray together and to hear a sermon from a leading member of the Muslim community. This kind of mosque, known in Arabic as *jami*, differed from a *masjid*, from which through Spanish the English word 'mosque' derives, whose basic meaning was 'a place for prostration'; a *masjid* could be large or small, a humble room in a hospital or barracks, or an impressive shrine. Later mosques were to be associated with education, healing, and death. Universities and schools, hospitals and tombs would enlarge the functions of a building originally intended for prayer.

In their Iraqi capital of Baghdad the Abbasids fused the religious tradition of Arabia with the cultures of ancient Greece and Persia to produce the richest compost of the medieval world. Al-Saffah's brother, al-Mansur, fathered a line of more than thirty caliphs, most of them to be begotton on non-Arabian, usually Persian, wives. Their effectiveness was steadily to diminish after the death of Harun al-Rashid (AD 809), the contemporary of Charlemagne and his superior in resources and culture. The Abbasids were not to banish the sense of disillusion which had brought them to power.

One reason for the gradual Abbasid decline was the way they treated their original supporters. Abu Muslim, who had put the Slaughterer on his throne, was murdered during an interview with his successor, al-Mansur. The Shia were persecuted even more thoroughly than under the Omayyads. Provinces of the empire were neglected.

In Cairo the canal that in Amr's time had ferried the cereals of Egypt to Arabia had fallen into disrepair, but it was still usable in late Omayyad times. Al-Mansur, the founder of Baghdad, closed it in AD 765 in order to spite some temporary enemies in Arabia. Thereafter the canal was merely to serve as an artery for the capital.

Abbasid treatment of their subjects—dictatorial and conspiratorial at once—undermined the bonds of trust between rulers and ruled. Arabian armies had already been discarded in favor of Persian; but since many Persians supported the Shia, they too were found unsuitable props for the Abbasid throne. Once again the problem of power, and once again an unsatisfactory solution.

This time the solution was a time bomb in the Arabic-speaking empire. To protect their interests the Abbasids relied on a new element in the Middle East: Turkish-speaking nomads who arrived in steady waves from central Asia. The Turks brought little but their ponies and ornamented saddles; their religion was an animism lightly overlaid by borrowing from the China on those western borders they had roamed. They were robustly built, devoted to fighting, and comparatively loyal. They were ready to sell their talents to whoever would pay. Absorbed into the culture of the caliphate, they became stalwart champions of orthodox—that is, non-Shiite—Islam. They were loyal to the Abbasid caliphs until, scenting their power, they preferred that the caliphs should be loyal to them. The slave became the master, the buyer the bought. The first large-scale buyer of Turks was the caliph Motassim, Harun al-Rashid's grandson. His burly praetorians began to quarrel with the citizens of Baghdad. The caliph decided on a bold move: he would transfer his capital sixty miles upriver from Baghdad. At Samarra he founded the largest metropolis since imperial Rome. Once again Egypt had a new foreign capital.

The gigantic Friday mosque, the chief monument to have survived from Samarra, symbolized the new situation in the caliphate—a situation to be mirrored in the provinces. The mosque was constructed so that sixty thousand soldiers could pray at once. Samarra depended entirely on these Turkish guards. To pay them (their upkeep cost two hundred million dirhams a year, or twice the yield of the land tax) and to sate the ambitions of their officers, the caliph and his weaker successors turned Islam into a feudal empire of farmed-out fiefs.

Egypt was one of these fiefs. It was offered, in 868, to a Turk named Bayikbey whom the caliph feared and wished to remove. (He soon had him murdered, in a gallant but ineffectual effort to stem the Turkish flood.) To farm the fief Bayikbey sent his son-in-law, Ahmed, to govern Egypt. Ahmed was the son of Tulun, a Turkish slave who had been sold to Baghdad and had risen to a leading position in the military establishment; he had displayed an unusual passion for Islamic learning which he bequeathed to his son. Ahmed (known to history as Ibn Tulun, the son of Tulun) was thirty-three when he arrived in Egypt.

The country had changed in structure and spirit since Amr's days. Physically, there was the new provincial capital of Medinat al-Askar. In building this second Islamic capital the Abbasids had hit upon the rule of all who have built on the east bank of the Nile: new cities must always be constructed to the north of the old. Practical reasons prompted this instinctive policy. Since the dominant wind was from the north, whoever built on the northern side of inhabited areas avoided their smells and dust.[1] Fustat in any case had disadvantages. The nearby hills shut it off from eastern breezes; high floods submerged its low-lying land; giant mosquitoes haunted its marshes and pools.

More important than the physical changes were the spiritual.

The bright dawn of cooperation between the Muslims and their Coptic neighbors had soured in the tax collector's harsh noon light. The needs of the empire (in particular those of the Turkish praetorians) had made taxes onerous. Monks, for example, were no longer exempt from the poll tax; a man sworn to poverty found money hard to raise. The documents of state were now kept in Arabic; the administration of justice and the collection of taxes were largely in Muslim hands. Constant revolts by the still Coptic majority had inspired the Omayyads to encourage Arabian settlers to move into Egypt to strengthen the Muslim element. The Abbasids, more ruthless than the Omayyads, had resorted to periodic massacres.

Ibn Tulun, sensing the mood of disillusion, aware of the caliph's weakness, decided to turn this fief into an independent state. (He was to wrest Syria from Abbasid control as well.) To show that his regime marked a decisive change he decided in his turn to build a new capital. He followed Abbasid precedent and chose a site a little to the north of Medinat al-Askar, extending from the hillock of Jebel Yashkur (where he planned his mosque) to the rocky spur of the Mokattam, on which he built his 'Dome of the Air,' a place in which to escape the stuffy atmosphere of the summer city. He built an aqueduct (the first of which we have record) to bring water to his palace from fresh springs south of the city. His city was known as al-Katai, or 'the Wards,' since it was divided into separate areas for various military contingents.

Ibn Tulun's roots in central Asia contributed little except his physical stamina and appearance. His cultural formation had been in the grandiose metropolis of Samarra. Something of this vanished capital was transplanted from the banks of the Tigris to the proximity of the Nile; its aroma survives in the written reports of Ibn Tulun's capital:

> The Meydan, where Ahmed and his captains played mall or polo, became the favorite resort of the town, and if one asked somebody where he was going the answer was sure to be "To the Meydan." It was entered by a number of gates, restricted to special classes, such as the Gate of the Nobles, the Gate of the Harim, or named after some peculiarity, as the Gate of Lions, which was surmounted by two lions in plaster, the Sag Gate, made of teak, the Gate of al-Darmun, so called because a huge black chamberlain of that name mounted guard there. Only Ahmed himself could ride through the central arch of the great triple gate: his 30,000 troops passed through the side arches.

With Ibn Tulun's passion for physical exercise went the administrative genius of the early Turks. (The Ottomans, more Balkan than Turkish, were to distort the reputation of the Turks, who in Egypt and Anatolia left magnificent public buildings as traces of considerable states.) He ruled justly and reduced taxation. At the same time he had the ruthlessness of a despot. "In sickness the fierce emir was a terror to his doctors. He refused to follow their orders, flouted their prescribed diet, and when he found himself still sinking, he had their heads chopped off, or flogged them till they died."

His son Khomaruya had tastes of the kind which such eighteenth-century writers as Voltaire and Beckford were to evoke in their 'Oriental' tales.

> He enlarged the palace and turned the Meydan into a garden, which he planted with rare trees and exquisite roses. The stems of the trees were thought unsightly and he coated them with sheets of copper gilt, between which and the trunk leaden pipes supplied water, not only to the trees, but to the canals and fountains that irrigated the garden by means of water wheels. There were beds of basil carefully cut out to formal patterns, red, blue, and yellow water lilies and gilliflowers, exotic plants from all countries, apricots grafted upon almond trees, and various horticultural experiments. A pigeon tower in the midst was stocked with turtledoves, wood pigeons, and all sorts of birds of rich plumage or sweet

song, who made a cheerful concert as they perched on the ladders set against the walls or skimmed over the ponds and rivulets. In the palace he adorned the walls of his 'Golden House' with gold and ultramarine, and there set up his statue and those of his wives in heroic size, admirably carved in wood, and painted and dressed to the life with gold crowns and jeweled ears and turbans. In front of the palace he laid out a lake of quicksilver, by the advice of his physician who recommended it as a cure for his lord's insomnia. It was fifty cubits each way and cost immense sums. Here the prince lay on an air bed, linked by silk cords to silver columns at the margin, and as he rocked and courted sleep his blue-eyed lion Zureyk faithfully guarded his master.

Khomaruya was able to support these expenses on an empire (conceded to him as a viceroyalty by the caliph) which stretched from Cyrenaica in the west to the Euphrates in the east. He married the caliph's daughter with as much expense as pomp.

But Tulunid Egypt did not survive the third generation. Khomaruya died in 896 and was succeeded by his fourteen-year-old son, whose name meant 'Father of the Soldiers of the Army.' The soldiers did for their adolescent father after an incompetent reign of six months. His brother Harun lasted six years before he too was murdered. By 905 an Abbasid army had regained control of Egypt.

The extravagant palaces of Ibn Tulun and his family, flimsily built and unrespected, perished in the vengeful reconquest. What has survived to commemorate a man whose practical skill went with a love of learning and art is the largest mosque in the Egyptian capital. This building, being dedicated to God, survived the hammers of vandals.

Ibn Tulun's congregational mosque was the third to be built in Islamic Egypt. Of the first, the mosque of Amr, much survives, but it is not what Amr built. Of the second, the Abbasid mosque, nothing survives. Though the minaret has been remodeled and the great ablution fountain in the courtyard added,[2] Ibn Tulun's mosque is substantially the same as when he completed it.

Ibn Tulun was determined to endow his city with a mosque worthy of an independent capital. For this purpose he employed a Christian architect (probably from Samarra) and expended 120,000 gold dinars. He obtained the money by no longer sending tribute to the caliph; he accounted for it to his people by claiming that he had discovered buried treasure—an excuse to be copied by later builders of costly buildings. The work was started in 877, according to one account, and was opened for prayers, as is shown by a commemorative inscription, in May 879.

The result is an architectural masterpiece which combines grandeur with tranquillity, majesty of conception with delicacy of detail. The influence of Iraq is pervasive. Ahmed and his father had worshiped in the Friday Mosque of Samarra, the grandiosity of whose containing walls looked back to the temples of the Babylonians. The first pre-Islamic feature of Ibn Tulun's mosque is the *ziyada*, or extension, which encloses external space on three sides of the mosque itself. (The fourth side, facing Mecca, was occupied by an administrative palace with a door giving onto the mosque.) This empty space removes the mosque from too close intimacy with the surrounding houses and corresponds to the sacred precincts of ancient Semitic sanctuaries. Ibn Tulun's cavalry may have used these vast enclosures to tether their steeds; the *ziyadas* were later used as bazaars; they are now cleared and provide an impressive approach to the mosque. "One mounts a slope to reach its doors, a few steps to enter the *ziyada*, and from the *ziyada* by another flight of steps to the mosque proper. This successive rise in levels recalls the Palace of Balkuwara at Samarra."[3] But the most vivid recollection of Iraq is the minaret. In Ibn Tulun's time the minaret was still a rudimentary form. The earliest minarets had probably been wooden platforms from which the muezzin summoned the faithful to their prayers; the pharos of Alexandria (which lasted until its destruction by an earthquake in the thirteenth century) may have suggested the tower form, since the Arabic word *minara* (the origin of minaret) means a place of flames, or lighthouse. The architects of the Samarra mosque had not imitated the pharos. They had instead created a giant spiral minaret which echoed, in a more elegant form, the tiered ziggurats (such as Aga Guf) which still puncture the Iraqi skyline and which in the ninth century were less eroded than they are today. A probably mythical tale accounts for the spiral shape of Ibn Tulun's minaret. The ruler, an impatient man who hated idle actions, was caught out in conference twisting a piece of paper into a spiral form. "Build me a minaret like that," he is supposed to have said, covering up his idle act. More likely he ordered his architect to build a helicoidal structure in the Samarra style. Later repairs have obscured the original design.

Echoes of Iraq haunt but do not distort a work of art which shows that Islamic architecture has come of age. The mosque proper consists of a courtyard, almost perfectly square, 302 feet long on each side, surrounded on all four sides by porticoes (or *riwaqs*), two aisles deep on three sides, five aisles deep on the side where the prayer niche points toward Mecca. The aisles which provide the worshipers with shade (and places of study or rest for the students and ascetics who in mosques have always found a home) are not formed from purloined Pharaonic or Coptic pillars. The whole mosque is built of red brick[4] and this brickwork is covered with stucco that is, on the piers of the aisles, molded into pillar shapes, each surmounted with late Corinthian capitals (still in stucco) where vine leaves of Samarran decoration have replaced the classical acanthus. The soffits, or undersides of the arches, are decorated with exquisite friezes of formalized plant design.

That this great mosque has survived at all is one of the miracles of Cairo; that it has been so frequently restored but not reshaped has made it perhaps the greatest possession of a city that possesses so much. It is significant that this aesthetic achievement was the product of the first independent dynasty in Egypt since the death of Cleopatra.

6

Fatimid Cairo
Awe Returns to Egypt

IBN TULUN, AS AN INDEPENDENT SOVEREIGN, contemporary
with England's Alfred the Great, and as a Muslim, offering
prayers in the name of the Abbasid caliph, could in his lifetime
reassure the people of Egypt that all was well. They admired
his buildings; they watched his polo; they cheered the military
victories that made the Tulunid capital the center of a considerable state. But the collapse of the dynasty, the restoration of
Abbasid authority, did more than devastate the proud city of al-
Katai. It revived the sense of disillusion which grew stronger as
the Abbasid caliphate lost its spiritual appeal and its cultural
vigor. At home in Iraq the rigid theologians had silenced the intellectual movements which had made ninth century Baghdad
so brilliant; religious men turned more and more to the interior
consolations of mysticism, or Sufism. Abroad, the caliphate
again lost its grip on Egypt, farming it out this time to a dynasty known as the Ikshidites (from the term Ikshid meaning
'king' in the founder's language, and conceded to him by the
caliph in return for tribute). This dynasty failed to revive the glories of Ibn Tulun and exacerbated popular discontent. It was
unable to protect the country from foreign invasions; it taxed
with severity.

The Shia exploited a feeling of world-weary disillusion by
adding to it a sense of milliennial hope. (Something of the same

mood was shared by tenth-century Christendom, where many people neglected their work in the expectation that Christ would return in the year 1000.) The Shia offered, not a return of Ali, but the emergence of a mahdi, an infallible ruler who would repair the ruin of Islam.

Only four years after the temporary restoration of Abbasid authority in Egypt, a focus for Shiite hopes was established for the first time in the Muslim world. Its improbable site was the province known to the Arabs as Ifriqiya (from the Roman 'Africa') and to the modern world as Tunisia.

How a descendant of Ali and Fatima (hence a Fatimid) survived the Abbasid secret police and created a kingdom for himself as the nucleus of an anticaliphate is one of history's great adventure stories. As in all true adventure stories—enacted in conditions of danger and double cross, maneuver and dissimulation—much of what happened is obscure. A brief outline can be given, but it must be remembered that each link in the chain may have been other than it seemed.

The man who headed the new dynasty was named Obaidallah. Of largely Persian extraction and culture he was accepted by the Shia as the great-grandson of Ismail, himself the undoubted descendant of Ali and Fatima. (Some branches of the Shia rejected Ismail because he had been known to drink. Those who accepted him replied that an imam was superior to man-made norms. By drinking he had not sinned but had shown that drinking was not sinful.) Obaidallah lived in prudent retirement in Syria, aware that he was the likely target of the Abbasid police. Just as the first Abbasid had owed everything to Abu Muslim, so the first Fatimid owed everything to another Persian energumen, a man surnamed al-Shi'i (the Shiite) for his devotion to the cause. Al-Shi'i must rank as one of the great propagandists of all time. Lacking modern means of communication, he used the best means available to him then: the annual pilgrimage to Mecca. He diffused Shiite ideas among the thousands of Persians, Egyptians, Arabs, and North Africans, who, having shown their sincerity by journeys of danger and cost, were inveitably men concerned with the deeper issues of the day. He had remarkable success with some fierce Berber tribesmen from what is now Algeria. (It is to be remarked that Shiite ideas have generally affected non-Semitic Muslims more than Arabs.) Al-

Shi'i was invited to accompany their caravan back to North Africa, ostensibly to teach the Koran but in reality to prepare the way for a Fatimid Messiah. No sooner had the Berbers got him back to their rugged mountains than they elected him their chief. To be a Berber chief meant something: almost single-handed a small Berber army had accomplished the conquest of Spain. Al-Shi'i used his new authority to effect. After a brilliant manipulation of conspiracies and tribal wars, he found himself in a position to offer a base to Obaidallah. Outwitting the Abbasid authorities in Egypt, Obaidalla reached Tripoli in North Africa. Captured in a preliminary setback, the man of destiny was imprisoned for three years by the orthodox dynasty then ruling Tunisia. But after his period of 'withdrawal' (so common in the lives of great men) he was rescued by the military élan of al-Shi'i who, on August 26, 909, presented him as the expected mahdi to a vast armed host. Al-Shi'i paid the normal price for his selfless zeal. The man he had enthroned put him to death less than two years later.

Like other founders of Muslim dynasties, Obaidallah disdained to occupy the capital of his predecessors. (This was Kairouan, the sister city of Amr's Fustat.) On a promontory off eastern Tunisia Obaidallah laid out a new city called Mahdia. This was a trial run for a new Egyptian capital which would be built toward the end of the century by the fourth ruler of Obaidallah's line.

Whether or not the original Fatimid had been a descendant of Ali or a masquerading Jew (as Obaidallah's enemies had claimed), the Fatimid conquest of Egypt owes much to a Jewish convert to Islam named Yakub Ibn Killis. Disappointed by his treatment at the hands of the Ikshidite rulers, Ibn Killis fled to the Fatimid court. He gave the current ruler, al-Mo'izz, precise information on the state of public opinion inside Egypt, as well as the weakness of its military defense.

The Fatimids had never envisaged settling for a small North African kingdom. They were far more ambitious than men of the stamp of Ibn Tulun. Their ambition was to take over the caliphate of Islam and reverse all that had happened since the death of Ali. For the center of a new caliphate (after Syria and Iraq) Egypt was a tempting choice. They had in fact attacked Egypt several times already. As early as 914 their fleet had taken Alexandria and their soldiers had occupied the large oasis of Fayum just south of the delta. The information Ibn Killis brought confirmed that many Egyptians were now looking to a descendant of Ali for deliverance; Ibn Killis assured the Fatimids that, unlike the other times they had probed at Egypt, this time they would not be resisted. The court astrologers, who greatly influenced the decisions of al-Mo'izz, affirmed that Ibn Killis had come at a propitious moment: the planet Jupiter had been in conjunction with Saturn in the sign of Aries when the Fatimids had taken over North Africa; it had now reverted to the same conjunction.

Prompted by military information and heavenly encouragement, al-Mo'izz put an army of 100,000 men at the disposal of a converted Greek called Gohar. His name meant 'jewel'; it was to be auspicious for his master. Leaving Tunisia in February 969, Gohar had occupied Alexandria and reached the west-bank suburb of Giza by early July. The optimism of Ibn Killis was justified. Egypt was not only defenseless but weakened by a plague; in the neighborhood of Misr half a million had died. After some skirmishes on the west bank, Gohar forced the swollen Nile and the capital threw itself on his mercy. It did not do so in vain. Gohar gave the inhabitants a complete amnesty, forbade his soldiers to loot, and led them into camp some distance north of the town. The spot where he encamped was on a higher level than Fustat. He could see, as Herodotus had seen fourteen centuries before, how "when the Nile inundates the country, the cities are seen above its surface, very like the islands in the Aegean Sea; for all the rest of Egypt becomes a sea, and the cities alone are above the surface. When this happens, they navigate no longer by the channel, but sail across the plain."

That same night, Gohar determined to lay out a new palace city for his distant master. The site he chose lay immediately to the north of the existing inhabited area, called collectively Misr. Except for one Coptic convent[1] and a minor watchtower, it was empty ground; the actual experience of the flood showed its height above Nile level. In the scene described (in the first chapter) Gohar laid out a rectangle enclosing some 300 acres. Its southern wall would face the populous cities of Ibn Tulun and Amr; its western wall would give onto the canal; its eastern wall would run parallel with the Mokattam hills; open country would lie beyond its northern gates.

Gohar's city was new in conception as well as site. It would deserve its epithet of 'the Guarded.' Its walls were enormously thick, made of bricks that were, in the Persian style, nearly two feet long and fifteen inches broad. Two horsemen would be able to canter abreast along the top. Gohar's plan, according to the Arab writer Ibn Duqmaq, was "to design palaces for his master to separate him and his friends and their armies from the general public." The new city was alien in spirit from democratic Fustat, where Amr had been a rough tribal leader among his soldiers, and alien too from al-Katai, where Ibn Tulun had reigned by the sword like some more civilized Anglo-Saxon king, enjoying the rough comradeship of his hedonistic knights. Gohar's sovereign was to reign mysteriously, as befitted an imam, from behind the curtain of awe. For Fatimid power was based on an idea: the sense that God allows an aspect of himself to be incarnate in an infallible ruler. Such a ruler must be hedged about with all that induces metaphysical and physical respect.

This palace city was to have a successor in the Forbidden City of Peking; it had a predecessor in the Dalmatian city (now Split) where Diocletian had retired from public display. The shrewd and skeptical Roman emperor had deliberately tried to fabricate an awe-filled atmosphere, hoping that the cult of an emperor deified, while still alive, like the Persian kings, might provide an ideological cement for a divided empire. Diocletian had failed because most of his subjects had begun to believe in the divinity of Christ, while nobody, least of all himself, believed in his own. The Fatimids had a stronger idea and were to propagate it successfully for two centuries. At least one member of the dynasty was to credit his own myth.

Four years after Gohar had started work the new city was ready for its caliph. Leaving a viceroy in North Africa, al-Mo'izz sailed to Alexandria and then traveled up the western branch of the Nile to the tip of the delta. He arrived in the month after Ramadan. The various quarters of the old city were beflagged in his honor. Completely ignoring them, the caliph drove solemnly into the palace enclosure. He was preceded by two elephants and the coffins of his ancestors. In Gohar's new congregational mosque, al-Azhar (the splendid), the caliph preached the sermon and then retired into the palace prepared for him.

Al-Mo'izz reigned only two years in his new capital. They were years of active accomplishment. The caliph was no palace parasite. He personally supervised every aspect of his government. He paid great attention to the army. Thanks to his sturdy North African troops, he was recognized as caliph in Mecca, Medina, Syria, and the whole of North Africa. Discovering that the old port of Babylon had silted up, he built a new one at Maks[2] farther north. This became the center of a lively shipbuilding industry.

It was probably al-Mo'izz who changed the capital's name from al-Mansuriya (after a city built by his father in Tunisia) to al-Qahira. The story of the raven and the bells was of the kind to impress his superstitious mind.[3]

At the same time al-Mo'izz set the sumptuous tone which was to characterize the whole Fatimid period, whose first century was probably the period of greatest Egyptian prosperity since the pharaohs. Apart from having a caliph in their midst, the Cairenes had someone who ran the taxes in a far more centralized manner than the previous tax collectors. These taxes, paid in a new Fatimid currency, allowed the dynasty to build lavishly and to patronize the consumer arts. The fortunes left by two of the caliph's daughters give a notion of Egypt's wealth. One bequeathed 2,700,000 gold dinars to her heirs; while the other's estate in gold, silver, embroideries, and precious stones required forty pounds of wax merely for seals.

The fact that the ruler could now be Egyptocentric, no longer sending yearly tribute to the Abbasid caliph in Iraq, benefited the ordinary people. The money stayed at home.

The founder was succeeded by his son al-Aziz, who reigned from 975 to 996. Al-Aziz retained the energy of a soldier while indulging yet more lavish tastes than those of his father. He had a connoisseur's knowledge of gems and when riding used jeweled harnesses scented with ambergris. His vizir was Ibn Killis, the same man who had advised the Fatimids to invade Egypt. Ibn Killis recognized that the only way the Fatimids could establish their caliphate was through education, or propaganda. He suggested turning the congregational mosque designed by

Gohar into something new: a teaching mosque which would be a powerhouse for Shiite ideas.

Al-Azhar was to remain for a thousand years the greatest teaching institution in the Muslim world, a religious university. But it was not to succeed in the task it was originally set. The majority of Muslims were not to accept the Shiite doctrines, which in Egypt itself made little headway.

The long-term failure of the Fatimids to convert the rest of Islam had important results.

On the international level, estranged from the Islamic East, which was loyal to the caliph in Baghdad, the Fatimids opened Cairo to the West. This was not the first time that Muslims and Europeans had met each other, but it was almost the first time they had met as equals. Harun al-Rashid had received ambassadors from Charlemagne and given the Latin Church authority over the Holy Places in Palestine; but these had been contacts between a high civilization and a near barbarism. By the eleventh century Europe was recovering from its Dark Ages isolation. This recovery was facilitated by contacts with the world of Islam, itself the repository of so much pre-Islamic culture. Spain and Sicily were bridges between the Christian and Islamic shores of the Mediterranean. Sicily in particular enjoyed friendly relations with Fatimid Egypt, both under its Muslim rulers until 1060, and then, on its conquest by Roger de Hauteville, under a Norman dynasty which admired and encouraged Islamic civilization. Trade in the island remained largely in Muslim hands while Arabs introduced sugar cane, flax, olives, and the cultivation of the silkworm into Sicily. A particularly Egyptian contribution was the papyrus plant, whose fiber provided cordage for ships. The court of Palermo was more eastern than western; Frederick II (who later became Holy Roman Emperor) wore Muslim clothes, had a harem, and regarded the Fatimid caliph as his closest ally. Encouraged by this symbiosis between Muslims and Christians in Norman Sicily, the merchants in the Italian city-states to the north traded eagerly with Egypt, a country not only rich in itself but the gateway to the yet greater riches of the Far East.

The isolation of the Fatimids from the rest of Islam had equally important results internally. The Fatimids could not trust their fellow Muslims. They felt safer using the services of

Jews, Copts, Armenians, Greeks, and other minorities. The activities of these employees, many of them extremely able, enabled the dynasty long to survive the deterioration of its members. Again, their rejection by other Muslims as heretics emboldened the Fatimids to defy the rigid prohibitions of orthodox Islam. Most Fatimid rulers drank wine, often enjoying the hospitality of monks in their vine-growing monasteries. They enjoyed feasting. For the furnishings of their palaces and the utensils of their feasts they ignored the growing prejudice against representational art. This prejudice had not bothered the early Omayyads or even some of the caliphs of Baghdad; Ibn Tulun's son had decorated his palace with egoistic statues. But the scholar jurists of Islam increasingly quoted a tradition of the Prophet (quite possibly false) to equate representation with idolatry. The Fatimids, arguing that the Koran made no mention of such a taboo, enlivened exquisite ceramics with lute players and animals. Their paintings, long since destroyed, are reported to have displayed the most lifelike semblances of secular and sacred scenes. In their public buildings that survive (such as the little mosque of al-Aqmar) there is an innovating freshness in decoration and design.

After fifteen years of Fatimid rule, Cairo had become the most impressive city in Islam, which meant, in the context of the tenth century, the world.

"Baghdad was in former time an illustrious city," wrote Maqdisi, the Arab traveler, in 985, "but it is now crumbling to decay and its glory has departed. I found neither pleasure nor aught worthy of admiration there. Cairo today is what Baghdad was in its prime, and I know no more illustrious city in Islam."

A road as wide as a parade ground separated the palace of al-Mo'izz from the smaller western palace of al-Aziz.[4] From afar these palaces loomed like mountains; near to, they could not be seen at all, so high were their walls. Giant black guards guarded an apparatus of state which revived the mystery of the pharaohs. It struck echoes of awe even in those who disapproved of the Fatimid ideas: at least while it had power to command and be obeyed.

The effect of this city on those inside its walls was yet more striking than on those outside. To be at the still center of this hieratic ant heap, to know oneself the heir of charismatic blood,

would have unsettled the most stable character. The effect on a
neurotic does not need to be conjectured—it can be seen in the
startling career of a son born to al-Aziz on August 14, 985, the
very year that Maqdisi paid his compliment to the glowing city.
The boy's mother was a Christian concubine of the caliph; she
was the sister of two Greek Orthodox bishops.

When the handsome child was a little more than eleven, his
father died. The third Fatimid caliph was given a good tutor, a
Slav called Burjuwan, and a sonorous official name: al-Hakim
bi-Amrillah, 'he who rules at the command of God.'

Al-Hakim has frequently been termed the Arab Caligula; the
comparison with Nero is perhaps more striking. Paradoxically,
there are also echoes of Akhnaton, the first pharaoh to be
known to us as an individual.

These echoes can be dealt with first. They are not religious:
the monotheistic innovations of Akhnaton were profound, those
of al-Hakim transient except for their garbled transference to a
Levantine sect. The echoes resound in the quality of individual-
ity shared by the two very different men inside a rigid and stylized tradition. The pharaohs were traditionally presented as
types, not as individuals; Akhnaton broke with this rule by in-
ducing his sculptors to portray his epicene expression and giant
female thighs. Arab historians of the Middle Ages worked in as
rigid a tradition as the Pharaonic sculptors and painters; it was
a tradition entirely different from that of Herodotus or Plutarch.
They made little effort to evoke the contradictory traits of character which compose great men. Two categories existed for Muslim biographers: the good and the bad. If a ruler was good, he
had the approved virtues of courage, generosity, sobriety, and
patience. If the writer disapproved of him, he lacked no vice.
This led to unconvincing biography. We feel intimate with few
great Muslims. The accounts of their lives that survive recall the
portraits of the Scottish kings which James VI commissioned for
the empty walls of Holyrood Palace. Only a moral monster (as
Akhnaton appears to have been a physical monster) could burst
such a tradition.

At this point comparison with the pacific Akhnaton ceases.
Those with Nero must take over.

Asked what had been the best period of the Roman empire,
the 'good emperor' Trajan named the first five years of Nero. It

could be argued that al-Hakim's reign (during which revolts in Syria were crushed and an invasion from the west ably defeated) was the high-water mark of medieval Cairo.

The young caliph was responsible for the embellishment and completion of a new great mosque which his father had started. It stood just outside the northern walls of Gohar's city. Now a haunted ruin, wrecked by misuse and earthquake, it retains enough vestiges to hint at an unrivaled elegance of taste. (Nothing comparable has survived of Nero's Golden House.)

Another comparison links al-Hakim with Nero. Just as Nero united against himself the pens of Christians he persecuted and of pagans he shocked, so al-Hakim's career outraged those who would write his obituaries. They were written without love. They bring him alive.

Al-Hakim wasted even less time than Nero in getting rid of his tutor. At the time he murdered Burjuwan he was a tall and powerfully built adolescent of fifteen. His actions were now entirely free. He showed signs of what would become an increasing obsession with night—an obsession shared by many lovers of Cairo—by instituting a nocturnal council composed of his advisers and intimates. The council was short-lived as the caliph soon tired of opinions other than his own. He now assumed total and meticulous control of the state and maintained this for the rest of his twenty-four-year reign. His entourage grew to dread his loud and resonant voice, to quail before his blue, dark-specked eyes. Those nearest him had most to fear. After Burjuwan he killed off other ministers of state. A victorious general who defeated the invading army of an Omayyad pretender from the west had the gratification of seeing the enemy leader paraded in a humiliating manner through the streets: he was buffetted from behind by an ape. Perhaps counting too much on the caliph's gratitude (or not sensing the caliph's interests in destroying a successful general), the general penetrated the royal apartments without due notice. He came upon a scene worthy of Gilles de Rais. The caliph was standing, his hands carmine with blood, over the disemboweled body of a handsome page. The general, of course, died.

Yet in his manic fashion al-Hakim came nearer to his subjects than many Islamic rulers. He dressed simply in a white woolen robe and disdained the panoply loved by less complex souls. On

a favorite mule known as 'the moon,' he would patrol the streets
of his capital inquiring into every aspect of public life. Sometimes he would summarily grant the petitions handed to him;
sometimes, if these were wearisome, the petitioner would suffer.
Caprice was the sole constant. Once an old woman was seen
standing at a street corner with what looked like a petition. The
caliph seized what proved to be a lampoon upon himself. When
he tried to vent his rage on the old woman he discovered that
she was a dummy put there by unknown enemies.

A series of decrees embodied the caliph's views. Many showed
animus against women. At one time he tried to impose a
twenty-four-hour curfew on the already secluded sex. He enforced
this by imposing a ban on the manufacture of women's shoes;
this he felt would be an effectual way of keeping them indoors
since the streets were often dirty and manure-strewn (despite
constant washing down by the army of water sellers). In the
struggle against alcohol he even forbade the sale of raisins, since
these could produce a fermented drink. He also forbade
malukhiya, a slimy vegetable dish popular to this day with
most Egyptians. One of his revolutionary proposals was that
day should be used for enjoyment or sleep; that night was the
time for work. The nocturnal Cairo which he loved now gleamed
with candles and lamps.

The people of Cairo had been inured to the whims of rulers.
(The first Ikshidite, for example, had increased his soldiers' pay
so that they could afford to dye their hair.) When the caliph
sealed and parboiled a public bath full of rowdy women, some
henpecked husbands may have nodded heads with sage approval. Even the caliph's personal methods of administering
justice would be approved by some. He took, for instance, a close
interest in the markets of his capital, always the focus of Arab
interest. On his rides through the narrow lanes of booths he was
accompanied by a tall, well-built Negro called Masoud. If he
found that a merchant was cheating he would command this
swarthy slave to inflict what Victorian proconsuls described as
"the worst indignity that one man can inflict upon another." Masoud would sodomize his victim openly in the man's shop; the
caliph did not disdain to assist by standing on the victim's
head. Masoud entered the folklore of Cairo. "If you won't stop," a
man would jokingly tell another, "I'll bring you Masoud."

Less tolerable was the drift of al-Hakim's thought.

It was a religious age and the caliph brooded on religion. Although his own mother was a Christian, although his two uncles were patriarchs, al-Hakim became the first serious persecutor of Christians in Islam. Copts were placed under many indignities, such as having to wear a heavy cross if they went to a public bath. In 1010, as part of his mania against Christians, he first had the church of the Holy Sepulcher in Jerusalem destroyed and then gave the custody of the Holy Places to the Greek church of his mother instead of the Latin church of western Europe. This interference in ecclesiastical affairs was to be a remote cause of the First Crusade later in the century. Yet thanks to his alienation from the majority of his own community, he continued to rely on Christians and Jews, despite his attempts to organize the mass conversion of both these groups. His feverish attempt to promote the Shiite cause convinced few Egyptians. But as a by-product of his missionary aim, the caliph achieved much for learning. He instituted a House of Science near his own palace where the learned could discuss every subject under the sun. It was probably the freest place of intellectual inquiry in the world at the time: the Shiites would open philosophical questions closed to the orthodox. Al-Hakim's library, planned as an intellectual arsenal, was one of the richest collections of Arabic manuscripts of all time. An observatory, intended to give astrological hints to the superstitious caliph, was in its meticulous equipment the forerunner of the scientific observatories of today.

If the Egyptians were little moved by Shiite theories, this was not the case with himself.

Awe from the cradle, caliphal authority from the age of eleven, absolute power from the age of fifteen, made a mounting assault on whatever of modesty or restraint still lurked behind his terrifying eyes. All his life, al-Hakim had been imbued with extremist fancies. One of the best known Shiite stories related how when the Prophet of God was assumed into heaven—his Night Journey was supposed to have started from the Rock in Jerusalem—he entered a vast hall at one end of which was the Inscrutable's throne. On the Prophet's entry a veil slid across the throne alcove—but not before the Prophet had seen that the hand drawing the curtain was the hand of Ali. Other Shiites argued that the Angel Gabriel had made a mistake of identification. Sent to summon Ali, he had summoned Muhammad to prophethood instead. Others argued that prophets were secondary to the avatars of deity whom they came to announce. As John the Baptist had announced his cousin Christ, so Muhammad had announced his cousin Ali.

The term avatar, derived from Aryan India, is used advisedly. Aryan Persia was to produce the greatest Muslim mystics and the most impassioned cultists of Ali. When al-Hakim's reason was tottering between prudence and insanity, two would-be prophets for an avatar arrived in Cairo. Both were Persians. They were to push an unreluctant caliph towards self-deification.

The first enthusiast was an unsuccessful feltmaker named Hamza. He was drawn to Cairo by reports of the intellectual debates there raging. At first he contented himself with arguing for al-Hakim's divinity in private; by 1017 he was bold enough to proclaim it openly. He made a forceful impact on a city crowded with genuine seekers after truth and plausible impostors greedy for caliphal subsidies. Hamza used a mosque for his pulpit. To growing cosmopolitan crowds he argued that al-Hakim, no ordinary man, was the incarnation of divinity. Hamza acquired the title 'Savior of Those Who Respond' and a considerable following. In return he provided al-Hakim too with a new title: 'The Maker of Time.' Al-Hakim took to visiting the mosque, which lay to the north of his palace city, and discussing Hamza's ideas. Aware that the majority of native Egyptians were shocked by notions which contradicted the basic unitarianism of Islam, al-Hakim provided Hamza and his disciples with arms for their self-defense. The need for such precautions was shown when one of these disciples, al-Akhram, was murdered while riding in the caliph's train. His murderer, an orthodox Muslim, was given a far larger funeral procession than the victim, despite the caliph's orders.

The second great advocate of al-Hakim's divinity was Muhammad Ibn Ismail al-Durzi. Al-Durzi started as a disciple of Hamza but like many extremists soon turned on his master. Hamza's teachings were carried to yet wilder extremes. According to al-Durzi, the soul of the first Adam had been reborn in Ali; this same soul had now returned in al-Hakim, the worthiest of Ali's descendants. Al-Durzi was entitled by his followers

'Supporter of God.' This new version of the Shiite doctrine was taken up by the usual retinue of time servers and flatterers. They took to addressing the caliph as 'Our Sole Lord, Giver of Life and Giver of Death.'

The anger of the ordinary people remained mute until the clash with what they had been taught in the Koran became too overt. A public scene roused the people to open rebellion.

One day in 1020 a group of Hamza's disciples entered Amr's mosque without dismounting—itself an impious and blasphemous act. The great courtyard was packed with people awaiting the chief judge of orthodox Islam. Three of the missionaries announced that they would take his place. They at once began expounding their thesis of the divine ruler sent from God. The people began to chant in reply the ancient battle cry: "God is greatest and He has no partners." At this moment the orthodox judge arrived with an escort of hundreds. The fervent Shiites handed him a paper to read. It opened with a parody of the usual *bismillah*: "In the Name of al-Hakim Billah, the merciful, the compassionate." This was too much for orthodox sensibility. The three fanatics were done to death on the spot.

Al-Hakim's response was worthy of Nero. He ordered his black slaves as well as his Turkish and Berber troops to loot the city. The soldiers were torn between their religious prejudices (which were with the people) and their cravings for loot (which were not). For three days the southern city blazed. Al-Hakim watched the spectacle from the grandstand of the Mokattam hills. His mania was characterized by violent mood swings. One moment he was jubilant at the pyres of smoke and the screams of victims; the next moment he was struck with compassion for those whom God had cursed. The holocaust ended when the regular troops sided with the people and insisted they would burn down the palace city unless al-Hakim called off his slaves.

Al-Hakim's death was a mysterious aftermath of this event. He had always been fond of solitary rides on the Mokattam hills. From one of these he did not return. It was debated whether he was killed by his relatives, afraid that in his madness he might bequeath the caliphate outside their circle, or by subjects goaded beyond endurance by caliphal caprice. To al-Durzi the fact that the mule was found without its master was proof that the avatar had returned to heaven. He successfully preached this doctrine in Syria where to this day the Druzes perpetuate al-Durzi's name and in their secretive doctrines the cult of his master.

Even personalities as bizarre as al-Hakim could only to a limited extent affect the collective life of Egypt. Though al-Hakim's son was weak and his grandson weaker, the prosperity of the Fatimid state enabled it to support great burdens; though years of drought were accompanied by speculation in corn and followed by epidemics and civil disturbance, they were succeeded by periods of rapid recovery. The country's agricultural wealth enabled the destroyed to be rebuilt and the weak to be repaired.

As late as 1047 Cairo was able not merely to impress but to convert an outstanding visitor.

Nasir Khosrau, whose life (1004–1088) more or less spanned the eleventh century, was a Persian scholar of the kind which Islamic education at its best would sometimes produce. He had memorized the Koran (which is about as long as the New Testament) by the time he was nine; it had taken him the next five years to master classical Arabic grammar, lexicology, and poetry; his early adolescence was devoted to astronomy and geometry, as well as to divining by sand and predicting by the stars. From fourteen to eighteen he studied the intricacies of Islamic law. His theoretical education was followed by a period of residence in India. Besides his native Persian and the official Arabic, the languages he knew included Turkish, Greek, the dialects of northwest India, and, in all probability, Hebrew.

Nasir visited Egypt in 1047. The caliph in power was al-Hakim's grandson, al-Mostansir. His capital was a double city: the northern palace city, al-Qahira, faced on its southern side the city of Misr, where the people lived and worked. Al-Qahira was impressive and Misr prosperous.

Nasir's account brings Fatimid Misr alive as a city bustling with life, its fifteen mosques maintained and crowded and its countless markets crammed with every form of produce. The caliph's insane grandfather had himself purchased both the two great mosques of Misr—the mosque of Amr and the mosque of Ibn Tulun—from the indigent descendants of their founders. (Mosques and other pious endowments could be inherited.) Al-Hakim had paid 30,000 dinars for the mosque of Ibn Tulun; he had added another 5,000 for the minaret when the family made as though they would otherwise pull it down. He paid a larger price—100,000 dinars—for the mosque of Amr. This mosque in particular was the focus of the spiritual and intellectual life of the city. There were seldom fewer than 5,000 people within its greatly expanded walls. On ordinary nights 100 lamps illuminated the mosque; on the nights of feasts no fewer than 700. The students, ascetics, travelers, and public writers who made it their haunt had aesthetic and intellectual distractions. Recitations of the Koran and religious discussions took place in the mosque's great courtyard; the eastern area roofed for prayer was now a forest of columns. The wall near the prayer niche was covered with white marble plaques on which the whole of the Koran had been inscribed in elegant calligraphy. The outside walls of the giant mosque were surrounded by *souqs*, or bazaars.

The vegetable variety sold in these *souqs* astounded the Persian visitor. On one single day—it can be precisely dated as December 18, 1048—Nasir recorded that he had seen in the market stalls: red roses, jasmine, water lilies, narcissi; bitter and sweet oranges, lemons, apples, melons, bananas, fresh cherry plums, fresh dates, raisins; sugar cane, aubergines, marrows, mangel-wurzels, turnips, celery, fresh broad beans, cucumbers, onions, garlic, beetroots, and carrots. It astonished Nasir that all these could be available on the same day in the same season.

The dwellings of Misr were no less impressive. Many were remarkably high. Nasir noticed that those which had seven stories were common, while some had as many as fourteen. There were terrace gardens on many roofs. One householder had solved the problem of watering his seventh-floor terrace in an ingenious manner. He had taken a young calf onto the roof, which had in due course grown into a bull; this stalwart creature turned an engine which raised the water required for a garden growing not only flowers and odorous shrubs, but orange trees and bananas.

Communications in the twin city were excellent. A bridge of thirty-six boats linked Roda Island to the east bank; from Roda a ferry service took the traveler to Giza on the west bank, where a famous Sunday market attracted huge crowds. Inside the city everyone rode mules or donkeys. Fifty thousand beasts which were available for a small fee were kept tethered all over the

city. Only soldiers rode horses. The Nile was used for pleasure.
Its banks were lined with kiosks and pavilions where one could
sit drinking freshly drawn water, listening to music, and admir-
ing the sunset. The caliph himself kept a 'stable' (Nasir's
metaphor) of twenty-one boats on a lake near his palace.

The prosperity was buttressed by a sense of security. The
merchants, and money-changers of Misr did not bother to lock
the doors of their shops when they left them for some purpose. A
thin chain would be stretched in front and no one dared steal.

Nasir has left a detailed account of what was to be, till the
twentieth century, the most colorful ceremony of the Cairo year.
Each summer the rise of the Nile would be carefully watched.
Throughout the country earth dams would hold back the
swelling waters; in Cairo itself a similar dam would prevent the
water from pouring into the city canal (which no longer linked
the Nile with the Red Sea) until the propitious moment. Then
simultaneously, throughout Egypt and in Cairo itself, the dams
would be broken. In the valley and the delta the water would
inundate the land; in Cairo the flood would fill the dry canal
with fresh clean water.

> When the time for the ceremony approaches [Nasir
> writes], they erect for the caliph, at the head of the
> canal, a huge awning of Byzantine satin, covered with
> embroidery in gold and sown with precious stones. All
> the interior furnishings are similarly decked. A hun-
> dred horsemen can stand in the shade of this tent.
>
> Before the ceremony, over a period of three days, ket-
> tledrums have been beaten in the royal stables and
> trumpets constantly blown; all this is to accustom the
> horses to a great din.
>
> When the caliph mounts his charger, there are in his
> procession 10,000 horses with saddles of gold, their
> harnesses enriched with precious stones. The saddle
> carpets are all of Byzantine satin and *bouqalemoun*
> which is woven expressly, neither cut nor sewn. An in-
> scription bearing the name of the ruler of Egypt runs
> round these saddle cloths. Each steed is covered with a
> coat of mail or armour. A helmet is placed on the
> pommel and other arms are affixed to the saddle itself.
>
> This day all the soldiers of the caliph are afoot: ar-
> ranged in companies and distinct detachments. The

first is that of Ketami, who came from Tunisia with al-Mo'izz; I am told there are 20,000 of them. The second is that of the Bathili; these are people from North Africa installed in Egypt before the arrival of al-Mo'izz. They are mounted and consist of around 15,000. The third are the Masmoudi; they are black and come from Masmoud: 20,000. The 'Easterners,' so called because, Egyptian-born, they are mostly of Turkish or Persian origin, not Arabs, number about 10,000, and have an imposing aspect. Then come a corps of slaves bought for money: roughly 30,000. Another corps consists of Bedouin from the Hijaz: 50,000 horsemen all armed with the lance. There is another corps of 30,000 slaves bought for various services. There is also a troop composed from the sons of foreign rulers who have come to Egypt; they are not considered as forming part of the army. These princes come from North Africa, Yemen, Byzantium, the Slav lands, Nubia and Ethiopia. Also in the procession can be observed men of letters, scholars, a fair number of poets, all stipendiaries of the caliph. Not one of these princes of whom I have just spoken gets less than five hundred dinars as his stipend; some receive as much as two thousand Maghrabi dinars. They have no duty to fulfil but that of attending the vizir's audience, of saluting him and then of returning to their homes.

The morning of the ceremony 10,000 men are engaged to lead by the bridle the horses of which first I spoke. Preceded by men beating drums and blowing trumpets and bugles they move forward in groups of a hundred. A company of soldiers marches behind them. For this service each man gets three dirhams. Then come camels, charged with palanquins and litters. At a great distance behind the horses and soldiers advances the caliph. He is a young man of imposing appearance and pleasing expression, as befits a descendant of Hussein, the Prince of the Faithful, the son of Ali. He has a shaved head and rides a mule whose bridle and saddle are of the utmost simplicity, unadorned by silver or gold. His white jubba covers a long full tunic, as is the fashion in Arab lands: its value at least ten thousand dinars. The caliph's turban is a length of white material rolled round his head; in his hand he holds a riding whip of high price. Just in front of him go three hundred Persians, all on foot, dressed in Byzantine brocade, belted at the waist. Their sleeves are long in the Egyptian manner. They carry short spades and mattocks; their legs are girt with lengths of cloth. The man who carries the caliph's parasol keeps close to him. He wears a turban of cloth of gold enriched with gems; his costume is worth ten thousand Maghrabi dinars. the parasol itself is of the utmost splendour. This officer is the only person near the caliph who is mounted. To the right and to the left eunuchs carry pots burning amber and aloes. As the caliph approaches it is customary for the people to prostrate themselves upon the ground and call down heavenly blessings upon him.

The vizir, the chief religious judges, and a large throng of doctors and functionaries follow the caliph. This great ruler thus reaches the head of the Canal, the place, that is, where it will take water from the Nile. He stays on horseback under the awning for the space of an hour. Then he is handed a short spade which he hurls against the dam. This done, the ordinary folk attack the dam with shovels and picks until it yields to the pressure of the water which then floods into the canal.

The first boat launched on the canal is filled with deaf mutes. These are believed to exert an auspicious influence; the sultan sees that they are given alms.

The whole population of Misr and al-Qahira throng to watch this spectacle and to take part in innumerable amusements.

Fatimid Egypt seemed to Nasir the noblest embodiment of Islam. Everyone, he wrote, trusted the ruler; no one feared arabitrary actions from the caliph or denunciation by informers; everyone was assured of the safety of what he owned. In some cases what Egyptians did own was astonishing. Nasir met one Christian whose number of boats and general wealth seemed incalculable. In one year of poor harvest this merchant had told the caliph that his reserves of flour could, if need be, feed the people of Misr for five years.

Nasir was lucky to have seen Fatimid Egypt at the zenith of its power, in a year when food was abundant at home and when abroad the caliphal writ ran in North Africa, Sicily, western

Arabia, Palestine, and Syria. Nasir took away with him a glow-ing vision of how a descendant of Ali could transform a state. He devoted many of his remaining years to writing poetry which ex-pressed ideas deriving from his stay in Cairo. The authorities in his Persian homeland did not take kindly to this poetic propa-ganda, and he died as a hermit in the remote mountains of Badakshan. Nevertheless, this one-sided vision of the glories of al-Mostansir's reign was to have a long-maturing fruit. In the sixteenth century, an independent dynasty, the Safawids, were to make Persia the one lastingly Shiite state in the Muslim world. Public opinion in Persia had been formed by Nasir, the first didactic poet in the Persian tongue.

Yet Nasir Khosrau's vision of eleventh-century Cairo was in-complete. The latter part of the handsome young caliph's reign marked the decline of Fatimid power and the start of radical changes in the appearance of the twin cities which composed its capital.

At the time of Nasir's visit the caliphal armies were success-fully challenging the Abbasid caliph of Baghdad and the inde-pendent Seljuk-Turkish sultanate (which nevertheless recog-nized the spiritual authority of the Abbasid caliph) ruled by Tughrul Beg. Al-Mostansir's armies did not remain united. The caliph's mother had been an African, and the caliph's sympa-thies were said to lie with his Negro guards. There were there-fore constant disturbances between his black soldiers and his white. These weakened the defenses of the state and did much to disorganize the urban prosperity which Nasir had described. In 1068 a Turkish army invaded Egypt and captured Cairo. The great library which al-Hakim had endowed, as well as the caliph's palace, went up in flames. In a moment al-Mostansir and his family were powerless and destitute. If the Turkish general had not been assassinated the Abbasid caliph's name would have replaced the Fatimid's in public prayers and the dy-nasty would have collapsed. Al-Mostansir was saved, not merely by the assassin's dagger, but by the timely arrival in Egypt—an arrival which illustrates the extreme mobility of the Middle Ages—of Badr al-Jamali, a gifted Armenian who put himself and his Armenian followers at the caliph's disposal. He was made commander of the Egyptian armies; the Arabic word for armies was *jyush*, or in the Egyptian pronunciation, *gyush*, and this gave him the name by which he is known: al-Gyushi. Though Syria was permanently lost to the Seljuks, al-Gyushi reconquered Egypt for the caliph.

The form and spirit of Cairo were profoundly affected by al-Gyushi.

He altered Cairo's form by rebuilding the walls of Gohar in a manner which owed much to his knowledge of Byzantine fortifications. He also made significant additions. In the north he extended the walls so as to bring the great extramural mosque of al-Hakim within their protection. The two great gates which still stand are his work: Bab al-Futuh (the Gate of Conquests) and Bab al-Nasr (the Gate of Victory). A memorial of Shiite doctrine was inscribed over the Gate of Victory. To the Muslim creed "No deity but God; Muhammad is the Prophet of God" was added the controversial sentence: "And Ali is the Deputy of God." (Al-Gyushi's own memorial was a lonely mosque on the Mokattam hills; even in ruin it shows the Fatimid elegance.) To the south he increased the palace city by about 200,000 square yards by pushing the walls a hundred yards toward Misr.

In the spirit of the palace city al-Gyushi started a transformation which was to be completed only with the collapse of the Fatimid dynasty which he had done so much to buttress. By encouraging some of the caliph's most trusted troops to build themselves private houses inside the walls of the city he altered the quasi-sacred nature of al-Qahira. By encouraging them to scrounge their building materials from abandoned houses in Fustat he accelerated the decline of that large region of the southern city.

Many factors contributed to the decline of Fustat. The disturbances in the city, the Turkish invasion, had emphasized the defenseless character of its houses. Centuries of experience had shown the climatic and geographic disadvantages of Amr's city. The level of health was notoriously worse in the southern town than farther north. The main port of the capital had moved north to Maks, as the old port of Fustat silted up; the branch of the Nile between Fustat and Roda island was frequently blocked. In summer evenings dust (raised by the hoofs of mules and camels) would merge with smoke (raised by the furnaces of public baths) to form a smog encompassing the city like a cloud;

passers-by choked and regular residents suffered from chest disease.

As people began to migrate nearer al-Qahira, or to build houses within its once exclusive walls, so Fustat sank into progressive neglect. From the reign of al-Mostansir dates a new Cairo phenomenon: the existence of vast areas of ruined and abandoned streets.

Known as *kharab*, these derelict quarters spread like a cancer. Even in the time of al-Gyushi such insalubrious quarters, haunts of thieves and prostitutes, extended in a great swath between the Roda bridge and the mosque of Ibn Tulun. Al-Gyushi's concentration on rebuilding and strengthening al-Qahira doomed the older southern city. It was left to its own devices. Its ruins grew more extensive. By the early twelfth century the derelict areas extended virtually from the mosque of Amr to the southern gates of the walled city. From time to time efforts were made to repair what was reparable. In particular, the area between Bab Zuweyla, the southern gate of the walled city, and the Rumeyla square at the foot of the Mokattam (near Ibn Tulun's polo Meydan) was put into some kind of shape. But deep in Fustat, lane after lane, street after street, had to be walled off as its condition became dangerous. Only two motives would induce the caliph to visit Fustat: to pray in the prestigious mosque of Amr, or to preside at the festivities concerned with the summer flood. To facilitate such journeys a road called al-Azam was cleared through the ruins. Its sides were lined by high walls which shut out the depressing vista of collapsing houses. This high wall, which hid decay but did nothing to arrest it, was symbolic of the last stage of Fatimid power—or impotence.

7

Saladin
A Muslim Idealist

THE SON OF A KURDISH CHIEF was to do for Egypt's capital
what Menes had done for Egypt itself: link the north with the
south in a new unity. While Menes had united the valley with
the delta on the linchpin of Memphis, Saladin opened the palace
city of the caliphs to aristocracy and plebs alike and joined it in
a comprehensive fortified unity with ruined Misr to the south.
The linchpin was a new fortress city built on the spur of the
Mokattam hills where Ibn Tulun had built his Dome of the Air.
Only after Saladin can the Egyptian capital as a whole be referred to as 'Cairo.'

How Saladin took over Egypt deserves recounting in some detail.

The Fatimid dynasty had amply justified—in part inspired—
the later analysis of the great medieval student of politics Ibn
Khaldun.[1] The passage of three generations, according to this
acute Tunisian analyst, sufficed to reduce an innovating dynasty
to exhaustion. Ibn Khaldun wrote from a vast experience of medieval Islam; the states he knew well stretched from Spain
through North Africa to the Middle East. He saw the history of
his age in terms of dynasties arising from sturdy desert stock
and degenerating under urban temptation into palace parasites
incapable of taking those actions which might have prolonged
their rule.

79

Although the Fatimids had ruled Egypt for two centuries, not two generations, the family had produced no effective ruler after the death of al-Hakim. Their weakness had affected their internal power and the extent of their domains abroad. At home the constant riots between soldiers of different race had caused anguish and loss to the people of Cairo; only the stupendous riches of the Egyptian soil could make good the losses.

Abroad the Fatimids lost effective control of North Africa and Syria. Thus weakened, they had to confront a major challenge from Western Europe.

The actions of al-Hakim in destroying the church of the Holy Sepulcher, his support for Byzantine Christians as against the Latins, had alienated the Christians of western Europe (to the Muslims known collectively as Franks) who were in 1095 to launch the First Crusade. Their motives were, of course, more complex than a simple desire to repossess the tomb of Christ. Younger sons of powerful families wanted to possess themselves of estates or kingdoms; ordinary Europeans wanted to see the world while earning merit. By 1099 the Franks had seized Jerusalem and massacred 70,000 Muslims, to say nothing of Jews and eastern Christians. The expansion of the Crusader state during the twelfth century was as rapid as that of Israel in the twentieth. In 1109 the Franks occupied the north Lebanese port of Tripoli; in 1124 Tyre had fallen to their arms; by 1153 Ascalon, the last Fatimid toehold on the Palestinian coast, was theirs.

Muslim disunity played as large a role in facilitating twelfth-century Christian Zionism as Arab disunity did in facilitating Jewish Zionism eight centuries later. Because the Fatimids were Shiite, they were regarded as heretics by the orthodox caliphate; the Fatimids themselves disapproved of the orthodox tenets of the Seljuk Turks, who in Syria offered the only nucleus of resistance to the invasion from the west. The caliphate itself was too preoccupied with its own troubles (the Mongol invasion which was to destory it in 1258 was only the last in a series of Turkic invasions from the east) to bother about events on the Levantine coast.

But Egypt could not be indifferent to the loss of Palestine and holy places sacred to Islam. Throughout Egyptian history the possession of Palestine, or the existence there of a friendly power, had been important. The earliest settlement on the site of Jerusalem, long before the reign of David, had been Egyptian.

Egypt was equally important—as an enemy, friend, or vassal—to the kingdom of Jerusalem, which saw itself as being there to stay. If either of the contestants in the Levant—the crusading Franks or the Seljuks of Damascus—were to win Egypt to its side, the gain might be decisive. Each side had ground for hopes.

The Franks understood the doctrinal schism which separated Seljuk Damascus under Nureddin the Turk from Fatimid Cairo. Just as Queen Elizabeth of Protestant England could argue that a dislike of popery linked her country to the Ottomans, so the king of Jerusalem could argue that in the Fatimid regime, dependent as it was on so many Christian ministers, he had a natural ally.

The hopes of the Damascus Muslims were more firmly based. They knew that the Shiite doctrines meant nothing to the Egyptian masses; the Islamic bond between Damascus and Cairo was heightened by a shared resentment at the Frankish occupation of Jerusalem, after Mecca and Medina Islam's most sacred city.

This double pull from the outside reflected itself within the sagging Fatimid state. There were those who, against the orthodox Muslims of Damascus, would side with the Frankish devil (to whom they were already paying a yearly tribute); and there were the majority who wished to be done with sectarian squabbles and to deal a Muslim counterblow to the foreign settlers.

Two viziers, Dirgham and Shawar, disputed the remains of Fatimid power.

Dirgham, with sectarian courage, made friends with Almaric, the king of Jerusalem. He expelled his rival, Shawar, who took refuge at the court of Nureddin in Damascus. In 1164 Shawar returned with the backing of a Syrian army led by a Kurdish warrior, Shirkoh. On Shirkoh's staff was his nephew Saladin. The invading Muslims defeated Dirgham, who in his desperation pillaged the pious foundations of Islam (or *awqaf*) to pay for his army. Despite this sacrilege, or because of it, his army melted and he was lynched by the mob. (Dirgham's readiness to collude with the Franks against Islam, as much as his laying hands on the awqaf, accounted for this outburst of violence.) In a short-lived stalemate, both armies, Frank and Syrian, withdrew; each was now aware of the weakness of Fatimid defense.

Soon Almaric was in touch with Shawar, who shared his predecessor's delusion that he could use the Franks for his own ends. William of Tyre, a leading Crusader, recounts an embassy of 1167. The palace gates were still guarded by Ethiopians; inside, large courtyards still glittered with marble; there were enchanting gardens, shady pools, menageries of exotic beasts. Behind the luxurious façade was evident debility. Soon an army, half Frank, half Arab under Shawar's son, took possession of Cairo.

This fraternization between Franks and Fatimids exasperated Nureddin, who decided on the conquest of Egypt. His deputy Shirkoh occupied Upper Egypt while his nephew Saladin took possession of Alexandria. After another truce the Frankish king in his turn decided the time had come to take over Egypt. This time there would be no question of an alliance with local supporters. He would rule alone.

Fatimid weakness in face of this Frankish threat gave the old southern city its *coup de grâce*.

Al-Qahira was protected by al-Gyushi's walls; Fustat had no protection whatsoever. In a desperate attempt to prevent the Franks from occupying and using this *terrain vague*—whose ramshackle dwellings of reed or palm leaf squatted among the ruined mansions Nasir had admired—the last caliph ordered the city to be burned in 1168. The thousands who still inhabited its ruined quarters fled like doomsday dead arising from their tombs. The evacuation was disorderly; in the general terror it was each man for himself. The owners of mounts took advantage of the panic. They charged ten dinars, instead of the usual pennies, for a ride from doomed Fustat to the gates of the walled city. Twenty thousand barrels of naphtha and ten thousand torches were used to ignite what remained of the capitals of Amr and Ibn Tulun. The fire flared, smoldered, and flared again for fifty-four days.

The people of Fustat, an Arab historian tells us, remembered a somber verse in the Koran: "These towns, We have destroyed them when they have sinned and for them We have appointed a time of destruction."

What was destroyed even more finally than Fustat was the hieratic spirit of the palace city. The refugees from the fire were lodged in the mosques, schools, and baths of the royal enclave. They were never to leave the once exclusive city. They were instead to make it their capital. The bazaars of goldsmiths and coppersmiths would stand where an avatar of God had withdrawn from his people. The grandiose palace blocks, the superb parade grounds, the tree-surrounded villas, became the ground plan of twisting narrow lanes, of mysterious cul-de-sacs, which remains the nucleus of Cairo to this day. It was a city which would often put up with monsters but which would never make them gods as well.

Having burned his southern capital, having prepared the transformation of his northern capital, the caliph sent tresses of his wives' hair to stir the hearts of the orthodox rulers in Syria. This time Shirkoh and his nephew arrived in Egypt to stay; the Franks withdrew. The volatile Shawar was put to death and his office assumed by Shirkoh. He enjoyed it for two months only, dying in March 1169. Saladin now became vizir of two contradictory faiths: of orthodox Islam in Damascus and of Shiite Islam in Cairo. This balancing act was difficult in an age of faith. Saladin performed it for two years. But when, on September 10, 1171, it was clear that the last Fatimid caliph was on his deathbed, prayers were offered in the Cairo mosques in the name of the caliph in Baghdad. The dying Fatimid was not informed.

With very little stir Shiite rule had ended in Egypt. The people of Cairo, never convinced by the teachings of their North African master, went about their business as usual.

Although of his twenty-four-year reign Saladin was to spend only eight in Cairo and to die in Damascus (1193), and although his main achievement was in defeating the Crusader state, he was to leave a more lasting impression on Cairo than any of his predecessors.

As a personality as much as a ruler and town planner, Saladin impressed his contemporaries, Christian and Muslim, and for the people of Cairo became a legend. If al-Hakim could be compared to Nero, Saladin could be compared to the second and greatest caliph, Omar. "Himself neither warrior nor governor by training or inclination, he took on both roles because he realised that the cause of his religion required someone who could revive the selfless determination of the early Muslim caliphs. Unselfish, humble, generous, he provided a new version of the Islamic ruler which struck echoes in his contemporaries. . . . He was no simpleton, but for all that an utterly simple and transparently honest man. He baffled his enemies, internal and external, because they expected to find him animated by the same motives as they were, and playing the political game as they played it."[2]

The political game in Saladin's time can be briefly summarized. As in most ages, its goal was the possession of power, either for its own satisfaction or for the pleasures it could bring. Its means were not the manipulation of voters but physical control based on a standing force of devoted mercenaries. 'Mercenaries,' in the context of the twelfth century, needs qualification. These men differed in some respects from the riffraff of later ages who would sell their killing power on contract. They were known as mamelukes. The word, which in Arabic means owned or possessed, explains their situation. Boys, usually Turks, were purchased from their conquerors or parents and trained to be professional cavalry. In due course, having been converted to Islam, they would often be freed and given estates on which to support themselves and dependents of their own. The mamelukes gave their loyalty to their owner so long as he treated them well. They would follow him into rebellion or new alliances without any moral considerations. They would loosen their loyalty if mistreated or underpaid. As they were opportunists, soldiers fighting for professional not idealistic motives, their loyalty was costly to maintain. Their tastes were expensive; they liked jewels and extravagant clothes. A small fief could maintain but a small number. One of the motives for the constant warfare of those days was the acquisition of more territory to support larger forces.

Saladin's repudiation of this anarchic system was shown in his every action. He had restored the name of the Abbasid caliph in public worship because he wished thereby to reunite Islam. He reigned not as caliph, but as *al-sultan*, 'the power'; he had no pretensions to religious leadership. He refused to move into one of the Fatimid palaces and lived in a modest residence outside the city walls until his new fortress on the Mokattam was built.

The inspiration for his city—a departure from the work of preceding town planners—came from his life as a young man in Seljuk service. Syria and southern Anatolia were dominated by military citadels on projecting spurs of rock. The form of these defensible high places occurred to him when he pondered the problem of guarding his Egyptian capital against further inroads from the north. The spur of the Mokattam which he chose was preferable to the Mokattam itself (where only the tomb mosque of al-Gyushi stood in lonely silence, wheeled round by hawks) since this plateau was completely waterless. Inside Saladin's fortress deep wells led to drinkable water.

Saladin's citadel differed from the citadel of today. The northern portion was a veritable town whose narrow lanes contained stables, workshops, even cattle pens. It was a practical place.

The ruler's administrative nucleus, bustling with the activities of state, was to be linked with all the existing east-bank settlements in one huge fortified *enceinte*. The city planned by Saladin thus resembled a giant inverted triangle whose southern tip was at the Castle of Babylon[3] and whose northern base was al-Gyushi's city wall extended considerably to the west, past the canal, to Maks. At this time the Nile silt had added about a mile of terra firma to the east bank; the channel of the Nile ran more or less where the railroad station stands today. The area enclosed by Saladin's walls was about 3,500 acres, or ten times as large as the Fatimid palace city.

On the spirit of Cairo Saladin left the impress of another Seljuk institution: the *madrasa*, or teaching mosque. Saladin recognized that the fragmentation of Islam was due to the decline of its spirit. The best way to revive this spirit was by extending education, particularly religious education, to the masses of the people. After Saladin's time the schooling of boys began to form a main purpose in many mosques.

We have contemporary eyewitnesses for the Cairo of Saladin's day.

One was Ibn Jubayr, a pious Muslim who worked as secretary to the Moorish governor of Granada. Offered wine by his employer (the date of the temptation was 1182), he refused, whereupon the angry governor forced him to drink seven cups of the forbidden liquid. Seized by remorse, the governor atoned by filling the seven cups with gold coins. Ibn Jubayr used the gold to finance a visit to the Near East. He arrived when Saladin's citadel was being built:

> We also looked upon the building of the Citadel [he wrote], an impregnable fortress adjoining Cairo which the sultan thinks to take as his residence, extending its walls until it enfolds the two cities of Misr and Cairo. The forced labourers on this construction, and those executing all the skilled services and vast preparations such as sizing the marble, cutting the huge stones, and digging the fosse that girdles the walls noted above—a fosse hollowed out with pick-axes from the rock to be a wonder amongst wonders of which trace may remain—were the foreign Christian[4] prisoners whose numbers were beyond computation.

A hospital endowed by Saladin also impresses the Moorish visitor:

> The maristan is a palace, goodly for its beauty and spaciousness. This benefaction he made so that he might deserve a heavenly reward, and to acquire merit. He appointed as intendant a man of science with whom he placed a store of drugs and whom he empowered to use the potions and apply them in their various forms. In the rooms of this palace were placed beds, fully appointed, for lying patients. At the disposal of the intendant are servants whose duty it is, morning and evening, to examine the conditions of the sick, and to bring them the food and potions that befit them. Facing this establishment is another specially for women, and they also have persons to attend them. A third, which adjoins them, a large place, has rooms with iron windows, and it has been taken as a place of confinement for the insane. They also have persons who daily examine their conditions and give them what is fitting for them.

Like other tourists, Ibn Jubayr was even more impressed by "the ancient pyramids, of miraculous construction and wonderful to look upon, four-sided, like huge pavilions rearing into the skies; two in particular shock the firmament. The length of one of them from one angle to another is three hundred and sixty-six paces. They have been built with immense hewn rocks, arranged above each other in an awesome fashion and wonderfully joined having nothing between them that, like cement, would serve to bind them. Their tips seem to the eye to be pointed, but it may be that the ascent to them is possible with danger and difficulty, and that their pointed tips may be found to be broad and level . . . ." There was dispute what the pyramids were. Some thought they were tombs of early prophets mentioned in the Koran, others that they were the granaries of Joseph. Ibn Jubayr's conclusion: "To be short, none but Great and Glorious God can know their story."

As much as by the modernities and antiquities of Saladin's capital, Ibn Jubayr was pleased by its atmosphere of order and justice. The desperate Fatimids had imposed a tax on the pilgrims who had to pass through their territory on the way to Mecca. Those who could not pay it were cruelly punished. "Among the various inflections devised was hanging by the testicles, or such foul acts. May God protect us from the abuse of His decrees." Saladin had abolished all such "foul acts." The subsequent revival of prosperity was extending the city even beyond his walls. We hear again of Giza. "On the west bank of the Nile . . . is a large and important burgh with fine buildings called Giza. Every Sunday it holds a large market where many congregate. Between it and Misr is an island, Roda, with fine houses and a commanding belvedere, which is a resort for entertainment and diversion."

Another visitor to the Cairo transformed by Saladin came from the eastern extremity of the Arab world. Abdul Latif was a physician from Baghdad who won the friendship of Saladin and his sons. Like Nasir Khosrau, he was a man of science in the Islamic tradition; that is, though specializing in medicine, he also had a thorough grounding in language, literature, and theology. In Cairo Abdul Latif was, toward the end of his stay, to make the one advance from Greek medical theory achieved until the advent of modern medicine in seventeenth-century Europe.

Like Ibn Jubayr, Abdul Latif was fascinated by the pyramids of Giza. Their number had already diminished by the time of his visit. The smallest ones had been quarried for the citadel. "Their ruin was effected by Karakush,[5] a Greek eunuch, one of the emirs, and a man of genius. To him was entrusted the superintendence of the buildings of the capital, and he it was who built the stone wall which surrounds Fustat and Cairo, the space between the two towns and the citadel on Mount Mokattam. He likewise constructed this citadel, and dug the two wells which are found today. These wells themselves are reckoned among the wonders of Egypt. They were descended by a staircase of nearly three hundred steps."

But the main pyramids remained. The two great ones of Cheops and Chefren were compared by poets, we are told, "to two large breasts rising from the bosom of Egypt."

The third pyramid of Mycerinus is described by Abdul Latif as being of red granite; it seems to have been his favorite; its external covering was apparently still intact in the early thirteenth century. Abdul Latif gives a scientific explanation for the shape of the pyramids:[6]

> The single most remarkable fact presented by these monuments is the pyramidal form in which they were built; this form begins with a square base and culminates in a point. One of the advantages of this form is that the centre of gravity is the centre of the building itself. Since it presses on itself, since itself supports the whole pressure of this mass, all its parts bear respectively one upon the other, and it does not press on any external point.

The Abbasid caliph Mamoun, son of Harun al-Rashid, had gashed an opening in the great pyramid in the hopes of discovering gold. All that had been discovered was an empty sarcophagus. Robbers had been working long before the Arabs.

Like modern tourists, those who went with Abdul Latif wanted to see inside.

> Most of our party clambered through the opening and mounted to the chamber in the upper part of the pyramid. On their return they talked of the wonderful things they had seen, that the passage was so full of bats and bat dung as to be almost blocked, that the bats were as big as pigeons, and that, high up, openings were visible and windows, constructed, it seems, to let in air and light.

Despite this rather unappetizing account, Abdul Latif summoned the courage, on a second visit, to go in himself.

> With several others I entered the interior passage and
> penetrated about two-thirds of its length. But fainting
> from the terror I experienced as I climbed, I returned
> half dead.

Saladin's son, who inherited his kingdom and reigned from 1193
until 1198, was persuaded by his courtiers to demolish the
pyramids. He began with the red pyramid, the last and smallest
of the three. The sultan sent drillers, stone cutters, and ropers,
under the supervision of some of the principal officers and emirs
of his court, with orders for its destruction. They pitched camp
near the pyramid, and mustered from every quarter an army of
workmen whose maintenance cost a fortune. They and their
horses stayed on the job eight months. With all their efforts they
were able to remove each day at most but one or two stones,
and this at the cost of tiring themselves utterly. Some were
charged to move the stones forward with wedges and levers;
others tugged at them from below with cords and cables. When
at last one of the stones fell, it made a tremendous noise which
reverberated far off, shaking the very earth, and making the
hills tremble. In its fall the stone would bury itself in the sand,
thus requiring extraordinary efforts to free it. By means of
wedges the stones were split into several pieces; each single
piece required a cart to carry it to the foot of the escarpment,
where it was left.

> After remaining long in camp, and expending all their
> money, they saw that their labour increased while
> their resolve diminished; in chagrin and shame the
> men who had been entrusted with the task confessed
> themselves beaten. So far from accomplishing what
> they had set out to do, they had merely spoilt the
> pyramid and shown themselves incapable. These
> events took place in the year 593 of the Hejira.[7]

Just as no two tourists take the same photograph, so these two
observers—Ibn Jubayr and Abdul Latif—left different descrip-
tions of the Sphinx.

Ibn Jubayr, the Moor, writes of "a strange figure of stone rising up like a minaret in the form of a man of fearsome aspect. It
face is towards the pyramids."

This account contains one error of fact and two dubious judg-
ments. The Sphinx, so far from facing towards the pyramids,

faces directly away from them, staring toward the rising sun. To justify the comparison with a minaret at all we must remember two things; that the Sphinx was buried up to its neck in the sand (the sand was not to be cleared away till the nineteenth century) and that minarets had not yet reached their later slimness. Even so the comparison seems poor. In describing the Sphinx's expression as fearsome, Ibn Jubayr was almost certainly moved by verbal rather than visual impressions. The Arabic name for the creature was Abu'l-Hol, which means 'Father of Terror.' The Arabs who first named it so were probably themselves confusing the ancient name of Horus, the beneficent god the Sphinx represented, with their word for terror; r and l being consonants that are frequently exchanged.

Abdul Latif gives a different description of the thirteenth-century Sphinx:

> A little more than a bowshot from these pyramids is a colossal figure of a head and neck projecting from the earth. The name of this is Abu'l-Hol and the body to which the head belongs is said to be buried under the earth. If the dimensions of the head are a clue to those of the body, it must be more than seventy cubits long. On the face is a reddish tint, and a red varnish as bright as if freshly put on. The face is remarkably beautiful; the mouth in particular has a charming expression; it seems to be smiling gently.

When Abdul Latif was later asked what had most impressed him in Egypt, he replied: the excellence of proportion in the Sphinx's head.

It was as an anatomist—in a season tragic for Cairo—that Abdul Latif made the chief discovery of his Egyptian journey. He also experienced the effects of a constant older than the pyramids or their guardian Horus: the Nile.

In 1200, when Abdul Latif was lodging in Cairo, the river rose no higher than twelve cubits and twenty-one fingers. Although it had started to rise at the proper time, by September 9 it had reached its peak and this was far too low to promise anything but dearth. The resultant state of the unflooded earth was called by the Egyptians *sheraqi*, an adjective which might have one of two possible meanings: either it might mean 'of the east wind,' referring to the wind which scorches the earth; or it might

be derived from a verb connected with drying meat in the sun,
like pemmican. Either way Abdul Latif and the populace took
the omens as sinister. (In describing the all-important progress
of their river the Egyptians still used the old Coptic months. The
Nile usually began to rise in Epiphi, which started on June 25;
was at its strongest in Tot, which began in late August; and
then declined in Paopi, which marked late September and early
October.) This ill-omened year the watchful Cairenes had noticed a greenish tint in the water similar in color to the leaves of
the white beet. This tint grew steadily more marked; it was accompanied by a fetid smell which resembled sour beet juice.
People began to prefer the brackish water from the Cairo wells.
Abdul Latif, as eager to experiment as Sir Francis Bacon four
centuries later, collected some of the water in a vial. A green
cloud formed on the surface which he removed and dried. It was
recognizably an aquatic moss. The water which remained was
clear, but it still tasted and smelled foul. Abdul Latif tried boil-
ing the water; this merely intensified its unpleasant attributes.

Despite the impending catastrophe, Abdul Latif, a true scien-
tist, was fascinated by his aquatic moss. He knew of the ways
in which the Copts claimed to foretell whether the flood whould
be high or low. In Upper Egypt they would put a lump of clay in
the open on a particular night; in the morning they would weigh
it and from the amount of moisture it had absorbed would pre-
dict the flood. Others linked the flood with the amount of dates
on the palms, or the amount of honey in the hives. Still others—
and Abdul Latif was not prepared to contradict them—believed
that the study of the stars could be a useful guide. But his
moss, Abdul Latif was sure, gave the clearest sign. This moss
must form in puddles and pools situated near the headwaters of
the Nile. When the rains in central Africa were weak, then the
moss would dominate the river, as it had done that particular
year; only when the rains were turbulent could they wash away
the moss. In this one particular the Nile was inferior to the two
great rivers of Abdul Latif's homeland. The Tigris and the Euphrates pelted southward from the highlands of Anatolia; they
flowed fast and clean to the Persian Gulf. The Nile, on the other
hand, moved from a region of stagnant swamp.

Having made his scientific analysis, Abdul Latif now observed
the effects of a Cairo famine.

Once it was clear that the Nile would not flood, food prices soared. Those who could afford to leave Egypt did so. Whole families—another reminder of how mobile medieval man could be—set off for Syria, Yemen, Arabia, and even Morocco. Country people swarmed into Cairo. When the cool winter had passed and the sun had entered Aries (the first sign of the new astrological year), the effects of dearth began to show. The poor, always indigent, were forced to eat carrion, dogs, corpses, and even the excrement of beasts. (An alarming diet anywhere, but to pious Muslims particularly objectionable.) Far worse was in store. The sight of unprotected waifs began to tempt the hungry. The government had to issue a decree that those who killed children or ate their flesh would be burned at the stake. The edict was ineffective. "I myself saw a small roasted child in a basket. They carried it to the emir and led in at the same time the mother and father of the child. The emir sentenced them both to be burnt alive."

Shock and disapproval soon turned into acquiescence in what became an everyday staple. "I saw one day a woman wounded in the head, whom ruffians dragged across a souq. They had arrested her while she was eating a roasted infant they found in her possession." What struck Abdul Latif about this gruesome scene was the indifference of the onlookers. They had become as inured to cannibalism as twentieth-century readers to accounts of air raids. Gourmets began to discuss what recipes got the best out of human flesh.

As the famine advanced, so gangs of hunters began to supply the market. Country orphans, driven into Cairo by the death of their parents, became the prey of men and women alike. Not many offenders were caught, though women had less skill at avoiding arrest than men. In the course of a few days thirty women were burned at Misr after confessing to eating children. "I saw them lead one before the governor, having a roasted child suspended from her neck. They gave her more than two hundred lashes to make her confess her crime, but in vain. She seemed to have lost all the faculties which characterize human nature." The guilty were burned. Their flesh, having been already cooked, was swiftly put on sale.

Adults, as well as children, soon had cause to fear. Physicians would be called out to lonely, ruined houses, and then attacked.

A frightened midwife told the emir a ghastly tale. She had been summoned to a house and on arrival had been invited to partake of a strange-looking stew.

"What meat is this?" she whispered to a little girl of the household.

"Oh, a fat lady came to visit us," the mite replied. "My father killed her and she's in there, strung up." Through a half-open door the midwife glimpsed a butcher's shop of human cadavers. On this occasion the cannibal, being rich, escaped with a bribe of three hundred dinars.

Fat old men went in particular peril. One portly bookseller only just eluded the nets of a gang who hunted round the area of Ibn Tulun's mosque. Another gang practiced near the mosque of Amr.

Children, women, men: finally it was the turn of relations. The tenderest bond of all became, not a barrier, but an inducement to appetite. A woman discovered nibbling a thigh retorted: "Why not? It's my husband." And an old woman argued that as the child she was eating was her grandchild, there was nothing wrong: it was better for her to eat it than an outsider.

What devastated Cairo assisted science.

As a physician Abdul Latif had been trained in the tradition of Galen. His education had consisted originally of memorizing a vast number of the second-century Greek's treatises. Galen himself had never been able to practice anatomy because of the Greek belief (so well exemplified in the story of Antigone and her dead brother) that the soul could find rest only if the body was buried. The Greek taboo against dissection of corpses was shared by Islam.

The Cairo famine now provided an observer with thousands of rotting bodies. Abdul Latif took advantage of his luck. He inspected a pile of 20,000 corpses near Maks. "The witness of our senses is better than reading Galen, who is often evasive," he could now declare in a startling declaration of medical independence. He was able to refute the master on a point of anatomy. All medieval physicians, following Galen, concurred in saying that the "jaw-bone is composed of two bones which are firmly joined near the chin. What I saw of this part of the corpses convinced me that the bone of the lower jaw is all one, with no joint or suture. I repeated the observation a great number of times, in over two thousand heads. I employed all kinds of means to assure myself of its truth, and I never saw anything but a single bone."

To defy tradition, to place observation over the authority of Galen, required courage. This act of courage—one step forward in the struggle for the disinterested investigation of physical phenomena—was one result of the famine which in 1200 reduced urban areas to empty wastes. In the heart of Cairo a tenement which had lodged fifty families would now house only the four watchmen of the street.

This disaster shows two constants in Cairo's history: the recurrence of famine and, more important, the extraordinary ability of the city to recover from this repeated disaster. It is not as though the famine described by Abdul Latif were unusual. To quote the researches of Marcel Clerget:[8] in one half century—which might seem exceptional, but was not—there were brutal famines in 1179, 1181, 1193, 1195, 1199–1202, 1206, 1220, 1226, 1229, and 1231. But again and again the Nile, whose penury in one year had caused the damage, repaired it with next year's plenty. This cycle of dearth and plenty profoundly affected the character of the city. The constant deaths in the city (such as were described by Abdul Latif) both increased the area of ruin, or *kharab*, and encouraged new settlers to move into the vacant houses. Cairo was a magnet to its hinterland. This included not only the Nile valley and delta, but all Muslim countries. For now that Saladin had reopened Egypt to orthodox Islam, "foreign students began again to frequent the mosques of Cairo. . . . Professors from remote cities of Persia or even from beyond the Oxus met the learned men of Cordova and Seville."[9] Such scholars married Egyptian women; as a result the population of the city was constantly enriched with alien blood.

8

Tree of Pearls
The First Woman to Rule Egypt
Since Cleopatra

LIKE A VICTORIAN FAMILY squabbling over a will, the descendants of Saladin disputed his power. The objects they coveted were provinces and their arguments were swords.

The last princeling of this weakened state had the imposing name of Malik al-Salih Nejm al-Din Ayyub. This 'pious king, star of religion,' as his name meant, had imprisoned his brother in the Citadel and then fought the Crusaders in Syria. To strengthen his power base, Ayyub had purchased a formidable body of stalwart young Kipchak slaves from a Turkish-speaking area between the Urals and the Caspian. These mamelukes quarreled with the townsfolk of Cairo in the same manner as the caliph's mercenaries had done with the people of Baghdad. Ayyub solved the problem less radically. Instead of moving his capital, he moved his mamelukes. He lodged them in barracks on Roda Island, thus keeping them some distance from the built-up areas. Though of Kurdish origin himself, Ayyub seems to have been a Turcophile. For his second wife he took a slave girl of Turkish origin whose pretty name, Shajrat al-Durr, meant Tree of Pearls.

Ayyub and his mamelukes were finally challenged at home in Egypt by the Seventh Crusade. The leader of this crusade was Louis IX of France, a man inspired by militant piety; but the crusading kings who accompanied him were making a last des-

95

perate attempt to seize the land bridge to the East. They wished to undo the commercial effects of Saladin's achievement—the isolation of Western Europe from the East—and make it possible for Europeans to import Far Eastern spices without paying enormous dues to Muslim Egypt.

In 1247 the Franks occupied the port of Damietta. Ayyub, by this time dying of a mixture of cancer and tuberculosis, was unable to repel the invaders. His death left the whole delta open to the Franks. His elder son, Turan Shah, was off fighting in Iraq; his son by his second wife, Khalil, was still a baby.

Tree of Pearls derived from a nomadic society in which women rode unveiled and had equal standing with men. (The Turks adopted the harem, and its symbol, the veil, after their contact with the more civilized countries to the south.) Her energy and strength of will were now to make her the first woman to rule from Cairo as her capital. To give herself time, she spirited her husband's corpse from near the delta battlefield and concealed it in the mameluke barracks on Roda Island. Meanwhile, she gave out that his majesty was on an invalid's diet, which she conspicuously prepared. Her ailing husband wished, she furthermore announced, to delegate his powers to a generalissimo who would play the role of viceroy until his son Turan should return from the East. This generalissimo would be one of Turan's mamelukes.

At this moment the balance in Egypt hung between some form of hereditary monarchy and a state overtly ruled by whoever could muster military power.

The French launched an attack in the delta which surprised the generalissimo in his bath. He was killed in it. Another slave–soldier, Bibars, then showed his mettle by launching a brilliant counterattack. The Egyptian countryside assisted his success. A diet of corpse-fed fish gave the Crusaders stomach pains and scurvy; these were followed by the plague. Louis IX was imprisoned in a house in Mansoura.

Turan Shah had now returned to his Egyptian inheritance. His stepmother gracefully conceded it. She may have guessed that his vicious and intemperate character—so typical of the third generation in these active houses—would soon destroy him. This time the redoubtable Bibars distinguished himself by striking the first blow at Ayyub's son. The terrified debauchee tried, in vain, to escape by plunging into the Nile. One of the murderers misjudged the temper of the imprisoned French king (to be canonized by his church) by bursting into his prison to display the bleeding heart of Turan Shah.

The monarchy was effectively destroyed. Egypt was without a sovereign. Now sensing their power, but making an unusual choice, the mamelukes called on Tree of Pearls, widow of the late king and mother of his surviving son Khalil, to assume the royal power. They agreed to her proposal that her mameluke lover, the emir Aibek, should act as viceroy. To placate Islamic prejudice against the rule of women, she would reign, not as Shajrat al-Durr, but as Um Khalil, Mother of Khalil. As such she would strike her coins.

But because of the loyalty to the Abbasid caliphate renewed by Saladin, Egypt was not entirely independent. Its ruler owed spiritual allegiance to Baghdad. When the mameluke emirs asked the caliph, Mostassim Billah, for formal permission to appoint Um Khalil as their ruler, they got an angry answer: the Prophet of God had said "Woe to the nations ruled by women." If the mamelukes could not produce a man themselves, the caliph would send one.

The mamelukes thereupon appointed Emir Aibek as sultan, while leaving the exercise of power to Tree of Pearls, who was now his wife. Being interested in power, not its trappings, she was pleased with this solution. She was prepared to rule the state from behind a curtain. This hung in front of her special seat in the Citadel's Hall of Columns, the great reception building where the affairs of state were discussed and managed. From behind her modest screen she received ambassadors and commanded subordinates. In the Citadel, too, she instituted nightly concerts of military music.

The beneficent interlude between monarchy and a new form of despotism lasted until Aibek betrayed, not the queen, but the woman. Islamic law allowed a man to have four wives at once. The queen was aware that Aibek's control of Syria might be made less precarious if he married the daughters of powerful men in that dissident province. Her jealousy forbade her acceptance of such a scheme.

From his side, Aibek had begun to resent his wife's monopoly of his masculine attentions. Like many men of action he was superstitious. A court astrologer had warned that he would die at the hands of a woman. He prepared a plan to lessen his dependence on Tree of Pearls. An alliance with the emir of Mosul, who had a beautiful daughter, was his simple scheme.

The queen found him out. The way she did so gives the flavor of a system in which the minute hand was intrigue and the hour hand treason.

A group of refractory mameluke youths had been sent by Aibek to the Citadel to await his chastisement. One of them knew the queen and her jealous temper. As they stood, bound, in the hot courtyard, he recognized the window above; in its alcove the queen often sat. Suspecting she might be there, behind its meshrebiyeh grille, he whispered in the Turkish which the queen knew from her childhood:

"I am the mameluke Idekin; I carry the slippers of the sultan. I swear, Princess, we know not why we are held. But when his Majesty ordered us to go to Mosul to ask for the hand of the Princess, we expressed our indignation on your behalf. For to you and your late husband we owe all we have."

The fluttering of a handkerchief told the cunning youth that his mistress had listened and understood. As the mamelukes were led off to their noisome dungeon, Idekin reassured his friends. "The sultan has contrived our imprisonment; but we have contrived his doom."

The queen was decisive. She posted a letter to one of Aibek's enemies in Syria. "Learn this: after putting the sultan to death, I intend to marry you and place you on the throne of Egypt."

The men in this story were less brave and more garrulous than the women. The Syrian emir either feared that the proposal concealed a trap, or felt that the queen's proposals were those of a praying mantis. In his alarm he consulted the emir of Mosul, who in turn warned Aibek. A royal dowshah raged between husband and wife, relecting the affection that still linked them both. Aibek left his quarters in the Citadel for a small pavilion near the polo ground of al-Luk. This was a flat area of silt-formed land to the west of the city. He vented his anger on the ball. A few days later, after a vigorious chukka, he received an overture from Tree of Pearls. He was ready to make peace. Grubby from the game, he decided to ride to the Citadel and wash off the grime before appeasing his queen. As he entered the bath five concealed assassins rushed at him with swords. Like Racine's Hermione, Tree of Pearls could not support her own decision. Seeing her lover helpless, naked, hearing his piteous cries, she entreated the assassins to spare his life. With murderer's logic, one replied: "If we stop, Madame, half way through our job, he will kill you and us." They got on with the job.

The guilt-stricken queen was terrified. When her offer to marry the new chief mameluke was declined, she put it about that Aibek had died of natural causes. But palaces were gossipy places; murders were not easy to conceal. Aibek's personal mamelukes learned the truth from the queen's serving-women whom they briskly tortured. The queen was shut up with her jewels in a Citadel strong room. Somehow she obtained a mortar and pestle and in the brief time left ground her jewels to dust.

The mamelukes now recognized their power to make and unmake their ruler. For the next sultan they chose Aibek's son by a previous wife. The young man emerged from retirement to the delights of power. His first thoughts were to reward his injured mother, who had been divorced at the queen's command. The dutiful youth offered her the queen to do with as she wished. The woman's revenge was commonplace but painful. Having insulted and stripped Tree of Pearls, she handed her over to her women. These angry dames beat the former queen to death in the bath; the tools they used were the heavy wooden clogs used in the *hammam*. Her battered corpse was then flung over the Citadel wall to feed the pariah dogs which haunt the desert parts of eastern towns. With that compassion which no less haunts the East, the queen's remains were collected in a basket and buried in the small mausoleum she had built for herself during her brief personal reign. It still survives. It has, in its prayer niche, the earliest example in Cairo of the use of golden and dark-hued Byzantine mosaic. Popular prejudice against a woman ruler—as in the case of Queen Hatshepsut three thousand years earlier—caused the deliberate defacing of inscriptions that recorded her rule.

The queen's short reign was memorable for more than the singularity of her funerary mosque.

Tree of Pearls had made the pilgrimage to Mecca in royal state. She had traveled, concealed, in a richly ornamented howdah. Too busy with problems of power to make the pilgrimage again, she had sent the howdah, or *mahmal*, empty of herself but containing the aura of royal power. The symbolism of the gesture caught the imagination of the people and their rulers. In its solemn procession it echoed both the Hebrew Ark of the Covenant and the ritual boats of the pharaohs borne above the heads of the people. Later rulers, beginning with Bibars, maintained the custom and the departure of the *mahmal* for Mecca became an annual event. The *mahmal's* shape was traditional. It was described six centuries later by Edward Lane:[1]

> It is a square skeleton-frame of wood, with a pyramidal top; and has a covering of black brocade richly worked with inscriptions and ornamental embroidery in gold, in some parts upon a ground of green or red silk, with tassels surmounted by silver balls. Its covering is not always made after the same pattern, with regard to the decorations; but in every cover that I have seen, I have remarked, on the upper part of the front, a view of the Temple of Mecca, worked in gold; and, over it, the sultan's cipher. It contains nothing; but has two mus-hafs (or copies of the Koran), one on a small scroll, the other in the usual form of a book, also small, each enclosed in a case of gilt silver, attached externally at the top.

A specially tall and handsome camel was chosen each year for the sacred burden; his reward would be retirement from all menial labor for the rest of his days. Those who saw the *mahmal* pass would rush to kiss its hanging fringes. In popular belief, to kiss these fringes was the equivalent of kissing the Prophet's hand.[2]

This peculiar custom would be enough to preserve the memory of Tree of Pearls.[3] More tragically, her reign marked a historical transition of somber import. Monarchy, in its various traditional forms, gave way to mameluke rule—to the despotism of white slaves who depended on other white slaves for their power. Mamelukes were to provide the sovereign rulers of Egypt from the death of Tree of Pearls in 1257 until the Ottoman conquest of Egypt in 1517; thereafter the mamelukes were to provide the country's ruling caste until they were destroyed by Muhammad Ali, himself a mameluke writ large, in 1811. In one sense Tree of Pearls was a mameluke herself: a Turkish slave, the paramour of the mameluke emir, Aibek. Yet she was also the widow of a free king. More important she had been a woman. A woman's caprice was not to rule Cairo again. The whims of men, no gentler, as capricious, were from now on in charge.

9

Platonic Republic Without Philosophy

Classical writers such as Aristotle had thought to define the possible systems of government under which men could live. Experts on aristocracy, oligarchy, and democracy, they never envisaged a system as strange as that whereby white-skinned slaves ruled a dark-skinned Egypt.

The Egyptians wrote about their muscular lords, retailing their foreign expeditions, their victories, their defeats; they described the coming to power of a fresh sultan, his donation to the troops, or the death of a tired one, no more able to donate. The feasts of a triumphant mameluke, the burial of a failure, bejeweled their pages. They made no attempt to analyze the system, nor did European travelers. These described the externals of what was, until the seventeenth century, "the greatest city on earth." They were fascinated by the recurrent spectacles of this mysterious place: the noisy departure for the pilgrimage, the joyous summer morning when the canal was breached. Like the Egyptians, the Europeans accepted the mamelukes as a fact of political life, hardly more to be analyzed than the weather.

After the mamelukes' extinction, European scholars such as Dr. Weil[1] or Sir William Muir[2] made efforts to preserve what Arab historians had written. But both were Victorian. At a time when western Europe and America semed to be nudging the world towards liberal democracy, when habeas corpus was as

103

exportable as top hats and railways, the underlying pattern of
the mameluke system seemed irrational and absurd: something
that had occurred once and would not occur again. Except for its
details, of color or cruelty, of excess or blight, it was as pointless
as the history of Scotland before its union with England: a sequence of power changes important to those who took part in
them, but insignificant as part of the progress toward liberty
and peace.

To a historian like Muir the mamelukes offered repugnant
problems, too. "Of their habits and inner life we have scarcely
anything as our guide. To one dark feature we can but distantly
allude." Muir published this in 1896, when Oscar Wilde had
just been jailed.

The twentieth-century writer has a melancholy new freedom
which allows him to mention sodomy by name; his experience
also persuades him that mameluke rule was far less transient
than his grandparents supposed. A widespread rejection of the
liberal dream, the rule of the muscle-bound under different titles, the erosion of constitutional freedoms, the revival of torture—such signs of modern progress make the mamelukes seem
our contemporaries. We know what they were about.

The mameluke system was never worked out theoretically and
then applied. Like other systems, it was the response to a complex of needs.

Islamic societies, distrustful of the loyalty or prowess of their
peasants, needed reliable defenders. The caliphate based on
Baghdad and Samarra had initiated the system. It was to find
its perfect field in Egypt whose covetable wealth required protection.

Need equally inspired the nomads who protected, then took
over, the fragments of a formerly Arab empire. The Arabians
themselves had migrated from their deserts impelled in part by
need. The migrant tribes which moved west out of eastern
Asia—tribes belonging for the most part to the Turkic race—
were inspired by need alone. They brought no religion, no culture
with them: only themselves. As they traveled through the uncivi-
lized areas on the northern boundaries of Islam they were—
again like the Arabians before Islam—equipped for a career as
soldiers by constant strife among themselves. They had no experience of settled family life; they despised (again like the Arabi-

ans) the settled, food-growing man. They saw humanity in two terms: the warrior nomad and the pacific farmer. The farmer should toil for the warrior or die at his hands.

From the thirteenth to the nineteenth century there seems to have been a steady overproduction of babies by these migrant parents. The pasturage of Asia, the pickings from intertribal war, seemed suddenly lean as travelers by their dung fires spoke of fertile Egypt with its many crops. They were inspired by tales of how Turks like themselves had become sultans or emirs. The supply of boy slaves became as spontaneous as it was abundant. No longer was it necessary for slaves to be acquired in war; parents were eager to sell their children into a chance of limitless wealth.

The spirit of Islam in two senses boosted the slave fighter's self-respect. God had ordained everything and every relationship, however servile. At the same time the relationship between God and man was that between master and slave. The *abd* prefixed to so many Muslim names emphasizes this bond: 'Abd-Allah' means, for example, 'the slave of God.' In colloquial Arabic, *abd* came to mean a Negro slave; the white mamelukes were not so described. Nevertheless, like the Negro slave, the mameluke was someone who had been bought by a master, for a certain task. It mattered very much to the mameluke's pride that he had been bought at a high price. Those who had cost a lot were proud of it; they often used their price in their title.

Bibars, the mameluke so prominent in the reign of Tree of Pearls, had been originally sold at Damascus for 800 silver pieces, "but returned to the broker for a filmy defect in one of his blue eyes." The only mameluke to establish a substantial hereditary line was Kilawun. He took as one of his titles 'al-Alfi,' or the Thousander, from the heavy price paid for him when he had been a handsome youth. (A great sultan was sometimes bought cheap. Qait Bey cost only fifty dinars.)

The system which grew up as though by hazard answered the needs of a society menaced by invaders from the north and east; it fitted into a society where the native people had long resigned themselves to being ruled by others.

The mamelukes were bought for the task of fighting, though the darker purposes alluded to by Muir must be discussed in due course. As cavalry they proved good investments to those anxious to maintain and, if possible, expand their kingly power. To the people of Egypt they were a less good bargain. But even for them they secured one advantage: when the Mongols devastated so much of the Middle East, under Genghis Khan and then under Tamerlane, Egypt was saved by its slave-rulers from the fate of Iraq. That Cairo has survived as it has survived—unlike Baghdad, whose memories of greatness are haunting fragments—was due to the mamelukes.

Much of what the mamelukes preserved was also their work. The most generous and persistent patrons of art that Egypt had known since Ptolemaic times, they were to create the distinctive skyline of Cairo, with its delicate minarets and tomb-protecting domes.

Liberal Arabists were long puzzled by what seemed a mysterious contradiction. How was it possible that such undesirable ruffians should have presided over an efflorescence of the arts that six centuries after its prime evoked astonishment? Stanley Lane-Poole[3] put it neatly in 1893:

> A band of lawless adventurers, slaves in origin, butchers by choice, turbulent, bloodthirsty, and too often treacherous, these slave kings had a keen appreciation for the arts which would have done credit to the most civilized ruler that ever sat on a constitutional throne.

Lane-Poole looked backward from his Cairo hotel to an England then at its apogee of greatness. On the British throne sat a dumpy yet civilized empress. What edifices inspired by Victoria or her late husband could be put against the buildings inspired by the mamelukes? "Their morals were indifferent, their conduct was violent and unscrupulous, yet they show in their buildings, their decoration, their dress and their furniture, a taste which it would be hard to parallel in Western countries even in the present aesthetic age."

The nearest Lane-Poole came to a solution of this puzzle was a passing reference to "the passion of the barbarian for display." Barbarians, however, were as plentiful as sand; only in Cairo had they commissioned such consistent masterpieces.

Other answers to the problem would have come, in the nineteenth century, from the exponents of the fashionable doctrine of race: men like the French Count Gobineau, or the English, later naturalized German, Houston Stewart Chamberlain. Such theo-

reticians would have argued that the migrants from central
Asia, in particular the Caucasians, were a more creative race
than the peoples they ruled. This theory encounters several hur-
dles. Neither the Turks nor the Circassians were precisely Indo-
European (the race usually favored by the racists); the artisans
who did the building and decorating of the mosques were the
permanent Egyptians, who rediscovered, under mameluke prod-
ding, the dexterity and taste which had distinguished the work
of their Pharaonic forebears.

The mystery of the mameluke achievement in art is a mystery
of taste, not a mystery of construction. The mamelukes were
themselves uncreative soldiers; they evoked from others patterns in stone, glass, and wood which are humane in proportion
and inspiring in effect.

Art and the love of art are deeply involved with man's emotional life. A solution to this mystery of taste may be connected
with that 'dark feature' which disturbed Sir William Muir.

The nearest Muir comes to confronting the dark feature is in
such sentences as the following where he talks of the jealous
dislike of one sultan (Nasser, the son of Kilawun) for his off-
spring: "Ahmed, the eldest, a wretched specimen of slavery to
the lowest form of vice, was banished to Kerak as his father
failed to sever him from the company of a mameluke youth."

The eighteenth century had been less tongue-tied.

The great French traveler Volney visited Egypt just before the
French Revolution, when a mameluke caste ruled Egypt under
nominal Ottoman sovereignty. At that time its area of recruit-
ment had moved from central Asia to the border provinces of the
Ottoman empire, in particular the Balkans. Most mamelukes
were the children of Christians; their parents had sold them for
profit. Volney was himself a domestic outsider. He had been
born a bastard and had changed his given name to an amalgam
whose first syllable commemorates Voltaire and whose second
commemorates the philosopher's residence at Ferney. From the
standpoint of a rationalist, Volney describes the mamelukes:

> Strangers among themselves, they are not bound by
> the bonds that bind other men. Without parents or
> children, the past has done nothing for them; they do
> nothing for the future. Ignorant and superstitious by
> upbringing, they become fierce through murders, muti-

nous through tumults, deceitful through intrigues, cowards through dissimulation and corrupt through every species of debauch. Above all they are addicts of that shameful custom that has been from time immemorial the vice of Greeks and Tartars: it is the first lesson they learn from their master of arms.

As a pre-Freudian Frenchman, Volney found it hard to account for this queer taste. The mamelukes were rich enough to afford women; indeed, they possessed them. He could only account for their vice by the supposition that a voluptuary lusts to experience from his own sex what he has inflicted on the other. But the vice was universal. "There is not one mameluke without this stain. Their contagion has infected the whole population of Cairo, including the Syrian Christians who dwell in the city."

In one respect at least—the fact that they were strangers among themselves, not bound by the normal human bonds—one is reminded of another institution which has patronized great art: the Roman Catholic Church. There the comparison must almost cease. The detachment of the Western cleric was effected by celibacy. The detachment of the mameluke from the usual concern for posterity was effected by two extraneous facts: the constant destruction of young men in deeds of violence, and the apparent inability of the mamelukes to found families which would last. This puzzled Volney. What prevented, he wondered, men of magnificent physique, married to sturdy women of their own race, from "adapting a blood formed at the feet of the Caucasus to the banks of the Nile?" He quoted an ancient Greek treatise (Hippocrates' On Air, Places and Water) to argue that Egypt was one of the two lands (the other was Scythia) where all the individuals were alike and where the race was quite separate from any other. Plants and men could not adapt themselves to such an idiosyncratic climate. This explained, for Volney, why instead of begetting replenishments, the mamelukes sent constantly abroad, to the slave markets, to keep up their numbers. (The mameluke indifference to the bonds of kinship is illustrated by a laconic paragraph in the biography of a sultan. "A little child was brought from the Caucasus who was said to be the sultan's brother; also another said to be the brother of the Secretary of State. They were both put in barracks.")

The caste's need for replenishment kept the slave markets of the eastern Mediterranean and the Levant busy. An account of the business was left by Emmanuel Piloti, a Venetian merchant from Crete who settled in Cairo around 1400 (it was he who styled it "the greatest city on earth") and lived there for forty years:

> There are in parts of Turkey and at the court of the Great Turk, as at Adrianople and Galipoli, several great heathen merchants who deal in no other merchandise than little male and female slaves of the right age to suit the sultan and to be brought to Cairo. When they have one hundred or two hundred souls, they take them to Galipoli and put them on shipboard; some are born from heathens, some from bad or ill-disposed Christians. They bring them, sometimes by way of Damietta, sometimes by way of Alexandria, and thence to Cairo. When they are brought into the presence of the sultan in Cairo, there are old practised valuers who are expert in judging a boy's appearance. They make great distinctions between one nation and another. Tartars are the most highly prized; they fetch between 130 and 140 ducats apiece. A Circassian goes for between 110 and 120 ducats, a Greek for ninety ducats, while Slavs and Albanians fetch between fifty and eighty ducats depending on quality.

Piloti puts the number of young slaves at the sultan's palace at between five and six thousand.

If the detachment of the mamelukes from family life parodied the Latin preisthood, their open practice of pederasty parodied Platonic ideals. Inspired by the 300-strong Theban 'Sacred Band,' Plato had proposed a Whitmanesque male friendship as a cement between the rulers of his republic. Plato himself lived in a society where most males had experienced, without guilt, attachment to members of their own sex. Without having the benefit of twentieth-century anthropological research—which tends to prove that practically any emotional pattern can exist in organized groups—Plato had foreseen one aspect of the mameluke system; the mameluke's indulgence in the love of boys Plato might have condoned; but while condoning he would have sought in vain for the philosophy which he commended as its accompaniment; he would probably have been indifferent (since, like Tolstoy, he disapproved of art) to the informed intelligence shown by unphilosophic soldiers where architecture and the arts were concerned. Twentieth-century psychology has given a clue which Plato lacked.

Latent feminity in a man—or masculinity in a woman—is often linked with an interest in art, or an ability to excel in it. A society in which men glide quickly from puberty to marriage, a society in which fatherhood is the main concern of males, tends to erode or conceal the feminine in a man. A society on the other hand where the first lesson a recruit must learn is to submit, in the feminine role, to another man, is a society where even the roughest develop whatever of the feminine exists in embryo within them. The mamelukes, for all their warlike mustaches and rowdy manners, were a caste deeply responsive to the arts which make life beautiful.

This is not to suggest that the mamelukes resembled pupils at progressive schools whose dream is an avant-garde canvas and its exhibition at a public gallery. The mamelukes were not artists themselves. While sensitive to beauty, they were more susceptible to the lure of power.

Most of the six thousand young slaves could hope for no more than a commonplace existence. The few who stood out could hope for a glittering if perilous career; there would be opportunities for acquiring splendid clothes, magnificent weapons, and handsome slaves. If a recruit caught the sultan's eye, if one of the emirs bought him for his own use or to offer to the sultan as a gift, he could rise through such menial roles as page, cup bearer, valet, or slipper bearer to formal emancipation and a position of trust. He could be made an emir of ten, then an emir of a hundred, and best of all, an emir of a thousand. He would then be in the running for supreme power himself, when his master died, if he belonged to the sultan, or, if he belonged to somebody else, when a sultan's debility or death opened the jousts to the cleverest intriguer or the toughest swordsman. As a senior emir his security would lessen as his prestige grew. Great wealth would in itself tempt enemies (including the sultan) to contrive his overthrow. If he rose to the supreme power, he could expect, as sultan, an average reign of five years and a few months.

No one has better described the mameluke mentality than Volney; though he diagnosed the caste in its decrepitude, his analysis of its motives and their calamitous results is as true of the fourteenth or fifteenth century as of the eighteenth:

> The young peasant sold in Mingrelia or Georgia no sooner sets foot in Egypt than his ideas undergo a revolutionary change. A boundless career opens before his eyes. Everything combines to stimulate his daring and ambition; still slave, he feels destined to be lord, and already he adopts the spirit of his future state. He assesses his master's need of him and sells dearly his service and his zeal; he weighs them against the salary he gets, or the salary he expects. And since this society knows no other incentive than money, the main preoccupation of masters is to gain the loyalty of their servants by appeasing their cupidity. Hence the profligate extravagance of the beys, so ruinous to the Egypt they despoil; hence this insubordination of the mamelukes, so fatal to the chiefs whom they exploit; hence the intrigues which never cease to agitate big and small. No sooner freed than a slave has his eyes on the highest posts; those who hold these posts have no moral superiority to inspire his respect. He sees nothing but soldiers like himself, whose power depends on the edicts of the strong; if the strong wish, he can arrive too. Nor will he be less skilled in the art of ruling, since this art consists solely in giving sabre cuts and taking money.

Power gained expressed itself in cruelty as much as in art. Two punishments in common use, according to the Arabic historians, were *al-tawsit*, in which the victim was cut in two at his belly, and *al-khazuq*, or impaling. "They stick a sharpened pale in the ground like a ship's mast. They lift the naked man onto the pale, whose point enters the rectum. They leave him for an hour or so, then finish him off by pulling him forcibly down." Flogging, manual strangulation, drowning in the Nile were simple punishments compared with the adfixture to a man's head of a metal helmet heated redhot. Though executioners usually undertook these gruesome tasks, an occasional sultan would intervene himself. Faraj, the son of Barkuk, for instance, spent a whole night killing mamelukes who annoyed him. One after another he cut their throats, and then dishonored their corpses with urine or wine. A man nailed to a board and paraded through the streets on camelback was a common sight. Such tortures (no worse than those inflicted in Christendom of the same date) reminded the emir that while art might delight posterity, only power could preserve his posterior from the agonizing pale.

For the great majority of mamelukes life revolved round the material pleasures available to men who lived in barracks, men who were brilliantly and briefly young, then obscurely middle-aged. They dreamed of acquiring enough money when they were in their youth to tide them through the years when no one feared them. The pay of mamelukes decreased as they aged.

Yet the white salves were not untouched by the spiritual aspects of the culture which they served. Piloti recounts what happened to the young barbarians after they had been bought. They were lodged in a great training establishment several stories high. Here, in airy dormitories, the pupils slept on rush mats. The school was under the control of respected eunuchs, each of whom had a class of twenty-five boys under his control. Before the mamelukes were submitted to the sultan—who would have his pick of the new generation on the occasion of the Nile flood—they were put through an exacting catechism in the religion of the Prophet.

There is no reason to doubt the sincerity of the mamelukes' attachment to Islam. Through it they subtilized their nomadic attitudes. Their undoubted passion for display was devoted to pious works as much as to jewels, furniture, and costly clothes. Though they still respected the profession of arms more than any other, though they still regarded merchants and farmers as inferior breeds, the Koran, which proclaimed that God had created men in degrees, gave them a sense of an overall pattern in human existence. This fusion of atavistic attitudes with the stately vision of the Prophet produced, under their swords, a caste system in Islam. It was a system that worked. It was a system that was accepted by those inside it. It was a system that resembled in some ways the feudal system of the West.

In this system, the Turks constituted the class that governed and fought. The cosmopolitan citizens of Cairo engaged in trade. The fellahin—for the most part Copts or the descendants of Copts—were those who produced food. The Bedouin were those who ferried cargoes across desert seas; they were also respected as fighting irregulars.

An important second class—immediately below the Turks—was the result of the mameluke belief in Islam. The sultan did not see himself as a man ruling on his own account; he held his power under God; over him and his subjects stood the Holy Law. As Islam made no distinction between the law of God and the law of the state, the purpose of the sultan was to effect what God had revealed through the Koran, the Prophet, and the consensus of Islam. This second important class was that of the *ulema*, or scholar jurists. They expounded and interpreted the Holy Law.

The mamelukes were orthodox in their Islam; they generally disapproved of the Sufi mystics; they actively persecuted the Shia of Ali. But to the four orthodox schools they gave public approval: the Hanifites, Hanbalites, Malikites, and Shafiyites. These schools were tendencies rather than sects. The differences between them were of nuance and tradition, more like the differences between various Catholic orders than like the differences between Protestant sects. A Hanifite would have no objection to praying in the mosque of a Shafiyite. One great mameluke mosque[4] was to have a schoolroom for each of the schools at the four corners of its central court. Each school was headed by its chief cadi, or judge; these four dignitaries played an important role in the public life of the mameluke state. Though the cadis and scholar jurists suffered, as a class, from timidity, though they were subservient more often than rebellious, they embodied an important reminder that the sultan's authority was not absolute. Even more important, as native-born Egyptians, they embodied a reminder to their foreign rulers of the potential dignity of those they ruled.

10

Mameluke Day

THE MAMELUKE SYSTEM WAS made firm by the same Bibars who had been rejected by his first purchaser for an eye flaw, who had counterattacked the Frankish soldiers in the Seventh Crusade, and who had taken a leading role in assassinating the last Ayyubid sovereign. Bibars was assisted by the greatest disaster in Islamic history: the sack of Baghdad by Hulagu in 1258. The Mongol victor, by murdering the thirty-seventh Abbasid caliph and his family, removed any spiritual overlord from the mamelukes of Egypt: by destroying the Iraqi canal system he turned the home province of the caliphate into a frontier waste of crumbling towns and neglected agriculture. Bibars led (under Kotuz, viceroy for Aibek's son) an army that defeated the Mongols and saved Syria and Egypt from the fate of Iraq. Bibars rewarded himself for his victory by murdering Kotuz; he then returned in triumph to Cairo, where he was unanimously elected sultan. His electors were the mamelukes who King Ayyub had barracked on Roda Island. Bibars was to control their allegiance for a reign of seventeen years. His energy as a military man and his justice as an administrator atoned for much of the violence that had put him on the throne.

Bibars was also a constitutionalist of vision. He was responsible for a legalistic innovation which made mameluke rule seem a right as well as a fact. He recognized that a slave sultan unsupported by any legal bulwark would be at the mercy of the first cabal among his fellow mamelukes or of any well-laid plot by those who would have liked to restore the Fatimids. Bibars hit on the ingenious notion of restoring the Abbasid dynasty of caliphs in his own capital.

The operation was conducted in two phases. "Hearing, therefore, that an Abbasid still survived the Mongol massacre, Bibars had him brought in triumph from Syria to Cairo. At his approach, the sultan with his court went forth in state to meet him, while even the Jews and Christians carrying aloft the Law and Gospel followed in his train. He was then installed as caliph, Bibars and the officers of state swearing fealty to him; while he in turn conferred on Bibars the sovereign title. At public worship, after the established ritual of reading the Koran and invocation of blessing on the Prophet and on the lineage of Abbas, the caliph offered prayer for the welfare of the sultan. Some weeks passed, and the royal party, having witnessed a festive combat on the Nile, assembled in a garden outside Cairo where the caliph invested Bibars with a robe of honour and the glittering badge of Imperial State."[1]

This was only the first phase. The intended puppet showed no understanding of the sultan's motives. Believing that his restoration was real, the caliph took Bibars with him to Syria with the intention of reconquering Iraq. Bibars knew that the caliph's gratitude might evaporate once he had secured a power base of his own; Islamic history provided too many examples of kingmakers being destroyed by their kings. Bibars therefore dispatched the dazzled caliph to Baghdad with a calculatedly inadequate force of Bedouin and Turks. The Mongol governor did the rest.

Bibars now moved into the second stage. A replacement for the dead caliph was produced who lacked his pretensions. A pensioner of the mameluke state, he embodied a shadowy continuity with the Islamic past. He had less real power than the Archbishop of Canterbury today. With the four cadis of the orthodox schools he formed part of the religious hierarchy of the mameluke state.

This state was effectively run. Bibars eradicated the remaining Frankish settlers from all of Palestine but the sea fort of Acre; having reaffirmed his defeat of the Mongols, he established mameluke authority deep in Anatolia. His imperial communications were fast. Letters between Cairo and Damascus took sixty hours—a speed not to be rivaled by the republican posts of the 1960s. The sultan himself was always on the move—"one day in Egypt, the next in Arabia; here in Syria, now in Aleppo." Under Bibars the empire of Saladin was pushed farther south. The Nubians of the Upper Nile valley were induced into Islam. Hitherto this dignified and honest people had belonged to the Coptic church.

Bibars bequeathed his system to a mameluke posterity; he could not bequeath it to his own. His son Said was "cruel and treacherous like his father, but utterly devoid of his father's ability"; he soon gave way to his father-in-law, Kilawun, the one mameluke to establish a line of descendants for a considerable time. Kilawun briefly posed as guardian of a younger son of Bibars, when Said was deposed; dropping the pose, he reigned as sultan from 1279; his last descendant was not deposed until 1382.

Kilawun spent much of his eleven-year reign in war. He possessed no fewer than twelve thousand mamelukes whom he regarded as a modern general regards his armored cars or tanks. He disposed a third of this armor, mostly Circassian, in a new barracks by the Citadel; the other two thirds remained on Roda Island. (The Arabic terms were *Bahri*—of the river, or the Nile—for those quartered in Roda; *Burji*—of the tower, or citadel—for those quartered at the foot of the Mokattam hills. The dynasty of Bibars and Kilawun is known as *Bahri*; its successors, who were largely Circassians from the Citadel, are known as *Burji*. The terms 'Nile Mamelukes' and 'Citadel Mamelukes' give the sense.)

In Cairo, Kilawun was to be remembered for the quantity of useful and beautiful building which he sponsored. One huge edifice, built by forced labor and with materials cannibalized from the pyramids and previous buildings, was designed to be college, hospital, and mausoleum all at once. As an educational establishment it included a library open to the public and staffed with librarians. Public lectures for adults were sponsored by each of the four orthodox schools. For children there was an orphanage, a children's religious school, and a species of kindergarten. As a medical establishment it had large rooms equipped with beds for the sick, whether rich or poor, male or female. There were well-stocked laboratories provided with every sort of medical appliance. The needs of the soul were not neglected: fifty readers chanted the Koran in the mausoleum.[2]

Kilawun's younger son Nasser, begotten when his father was in his sixties, reigned after his brother from 1293 to 1341, but not continuously. He was called to the throne on three separate occasions.

His first reign, as a child of nine, was very brief. After one year he was deposed by a Mongol mameluke, Katbogha, then kept deposed by a Greek mameluke, Lajin. The former was detested for introducing a tribe of horse-eating Tartars into Syria; the latter, married to a daughter of Bibars, and deserving well for his architectural works,[3] was despised for his passive submission to his minion, Menkutimur. He died by violence.

Nasser's second reign started when he was fourteen. Two great ministers—Salar and a second Bibars—now overshadowed him. Salar, a short, thickset Tartar with piercing eyes and swarthy skin, was his energetic regent; Bibars, a fair-skinned Circassian, was his economical majordomo. The young Nasser fared badly when he personally took to the field against a new incursion of Mongols into Syria. "The Egyptian troops, casting aside their arms and uniform, had fled from the battlefield in utter confusion past Damascus to Cairo, which the young sultan reached with hardly a follower about him."[4] He showed his mettle by taking rapid steps to undo the reverse. Egyptian counterattacks destroyed the Mongol power in Syria, pushed north into Armenia, and in the south crushed Bedouin revolts in Upper Egypt.

But closer to Cairo than forays on distant horizons was the devastating earthquake of 1302. It came in the middle of public rejoicing for one of Nasser's victories against the Mongols; the pious took it as a punishment for the drunkenness which had enlivened the feast. Suddenly the walls of the mosques began to tremble, houses to fall in upon themselves, minarets to sag like factory chimneys. Without their veils women rushed into the streets; the river hurled boats fifty yards onto the banks. After the earthquake the city looked as though it had been sacked.

Nasser's majordomo restored the mosque of al-Hakim; his polo master restored the last Fatimid mosque of al-Salih; Salar, his regent, restored the two great mosques of Amr and al-Azhar. None of the emirs spared expense. Salar in particular could afford to spend. His life of luxury, his love of extravagant clothes, were notorious. His daughter's dowry had been 160,000 gold dinars. His restoration of the ruined shrines reflected the complexity of mameluke rule: the coexistence of cruelty with piety, of barbaric display with exquisite taste.

Salar's chief monument commemorates a mameluke friendship which was lifelong and noble. His friend Sangar al-Gawly shared with him the cost and planning of a double mausoleum for them both which would include a school.

As though to show that loyal friendship could redeem even the power struggles of slaves, this tomb-mosque with its twin domes stands against a cliff which is all that remains of Ibn Tulun's military base.

Salar moved into this mausoleum when his brilliant career met a hungry end. In 1310 Nasser was able to enter into his full inheritance. In this third period of his reign he determined to destroy his two self-willed ministers, one of whom had reigned as virtual sovereign for a year. His experience of reversal had made him crueler. Jealous, suspicious, and avaricious, Nasser seems to have had an obsession with eating. He found it more difficult to forgive a remembered denial of food by Bibars, as superintendent of the palace kitchen, than his insubordination. Having made the usual promises of an amnesty, he had his niggardly majordomo brought before him in irons.

"Do you recall your answer when I once asked for a roast goose? You said: 'What will he do with a whole roast goose? Does he want to dine twenty times a day?' "

Bibars was first flogged, then carried to the execution room to be half strangled, then revived for one last scolding, then wholly strangled before Nasser's gaze. His property and slaves were divided among the rising mameluke emirs.

It was now Salar's turn to experience the vengeance of his phagomanic king. Trapped by the unwitting complicity of his dear friend Sangar, the mameluke millionaire (whose property, valued at 800 million gold coins, was not remote from Nasser's aim) was thrown into a dungeon. Enraged at the way he had been tricked, Salar refused a tray of prison fare sent down to him at Nasser's command. According to one account, Nasser retaliated by serving him a chilling diet: dishes of gold coins, silver coins, and precious stones were borne into the dungeons on sumptuous trays, under covers, as though to keep them hot. Salar died of starvation, having tried to eat his boots.

But unlike Bibars, whose body had been thrown into a sty, the body of Salar was lovingly washed and buried by his friend Sangar under one of the two domes in their joint mausoleum. Sangar would take his place under the adjoining dome twenty-four years later, having in the meantime governed Palestine, where he built monuments in Gaza and Hebron.

This concern with a fitting dwelling place for death linked the mamelukes and their subjects. The Pharaonic ancestors of the Egyptians had labored on their 'houses for eternity'; the Egyptians still buried their dead under the floors of what parodied ordinary houses. This concern with tombs was not Arabian. The Prophet's dictum, "the best grave is one you can rub away with the hand," was in tune with practice. Muhammad himself had been buried under the floor in his wife's hut; it is recorded of Abdul Aziz Ibn Saud, founder of modern Saudi Arabia, that ten years after the king's death no one in Riyadh knew where he was buried.

The mameluke concern with mausoleums may derive from Turkish awareness of the Chinese cult of ancestors. It is not likely to have been derived from Egyptian practice. For in India and Anatolia as much as in Egypt, rulers of Turkish origin built splendid mausoleums, of which the Taj Mahal and the early Ottoman tombs at Bursa are the most famous.

The Turkish obsession with tombs shows in the development of Cairo mosques.

The great early mosques of Amr, Ibn Tulun, and the Fatimids had been places for congregational prayer, for the hearing of sermons, for religious discussions. Al-Azhar had assumed the functions of a great college where scholars would lecture to groups of students by the pillars of the mosque; dormitories were added in which students from all over Islam would lodge, nation by nation, near their place of study. Saladin had introduced the Seljuk madrasa, or the mosque which was also a school.

Only as the Turkish element began to govern did the conception of the mosque as a tomb begin to dominate. This did not dissociate it from education. A school could still be attached to a tomb; the teaching of God's word could hallow the resting place of a man who needed forgiveness.

But there is an evident turning inward in these beautiful, melancholy mosques; the melancholy and the beauty go hand in hand. These mosques mirror an interiorization of Islam as Muslim ideals less and less affected communal life, as below the level of consciousness Islam recognized that the age when it held the future was no more. Mysticism, the contemplation of an inner landscape where the facts of history cast no shadow, was the consolation of the pious. A tomb became the consolation of the powerful. The greatest of all such tombs, built for Sultan Hassan, the seventh of Nasser's eight reigning sons, mirrors the mameluke puzzle. No shrine on earth is more calmly majestic. Four vast naves open onto a central court which rivals for religious awe the greatest of Pharaonic monuments; the chastity of its decoration—a great Kufic frieze of Koranic verses runs on a background of floral arabesques, the marble prayer niche is flanked by gothic pillars from Crusader churches—makes the later Pharaonic temples seem vulgar by contrast. Yet the tomb chamber holds a cenotaph. Hassan packed into a six-year reign (from 1354 to 1361) the usual quota of third-generation debauch. He died in prison and his body disappeared. The Citadel Mamelukes, who ruled Egypt from 1382 to 1517, sited their tombs at some distance from the city of the living. These mamelukes concentrated their buildings in the desolate region to the northeast and southeast of Cairo. In the northern cemetery, Barkuk, the first great Circassian sultan, is buried in a tomb built for him by his brutal son. It is even more remarkable than his mosque, built near the mosque of Kilawun. It stands in a khaki landscape, where no grass grows and where the wind whips dust against the stone of slowly eroding tombs. Barkuk's tomb-mosque is on the same pattern as Ibn Tulun's but the piers that support the cloisters are slender and the cloisters themselves are roofed with shallow domes. This mosque was not entirely abandoned to death. It was meant to be prayed in by congregations; attached to it was a retreat for scholars and holy men, one of whom is reputed to have been the historian Maqrizi; it also contained a school.

A short walk from this mosque is the greatest monument of the later mamelukes, the tomb of Qait Bey, himself the last impressive sultan. Painted by Bellini, he was described by Meshullam ben Menahem, a Jew from Tuscany, in 1481: "On Friday 22 June I saw the sultan close to. He is an old man of about eighty, but tall, handsome and as upright as a reed. Dressed in white, he was on horseback, accompanied by more than two thousand mameluke soldiers. . . . Whoever wishes can have access to the sultan: there is in the town a great and splendid fortress at the entrance of which he sits publicly on Mondays and Thursdays, accompanied by the governor of the city and his interpreters who stand at his side; a guard of more than three hundred mamelukes surrounds him. Whoever has been manhandled or robbed by one of the mameluke princes or emirs can there complain. Thus the nobles refrain from actions that might carry condemnation." A great builder, Qait Bey designed his tomb as a uniquely tall and solemn chamber set next to a small mosque for prayer. The minaret has the intricate, slim simplicity developed in mameluke times. But now that no Sufi ascetics live nearby, it calls only to the dead and those who live among the tombs.

For the ordinary Egyptians who were not yet dead and who planned no lavish tombs, life in mameluke Cairo was intermittently prosperous. Egypt was at the center of the trade routes of the world. While the mamelukes took much of the percentage, some filtered down to the merchants in the souqs. Despite the religious barriers between Islam and other faiths, Jews and Christians were politely welcomed. There could be exceptions to this easy policy. In 1335, during Nasser's third reign, Father Jacobus of Verona, a pilgrim who had already visited Palestine, Gaza, and Sinai, came to Cairo. His visit only lasted two days. There were rumors (unjustified) of a new Crusade. He had no time for more than superficial impressions:

> There are in Cairo and Babylon[5] numerous Christians known as Christians of the Belt; this is from the fact that they wear a belt while the Muslims do not. The Christians also wear black turbans, while the Muslims wear white ones. Otherwise they dress alike. . . . I saw a number of churches in Cairo, and would willingly have stayed several days to visit the marvels of the

town had not rumours of war—people believed that a new crusade was imminent—made people suspect that Italian or Latin Christians might be spies. I was very frightened and only stayed two days. With God's help and the assistance of some Christian slaves I escaped to Damietta by boat.

Other foreigners, such as Leonardo Frescobaldi of Florence, might get their facts wrong—he thought that the pyramids were Joseph's granaries and that the Citadel was the place where Moses had been reared—but could calmly describe the customs and costumes of the people. "It is necessary to know," he wrote after a visit during the reign of Barkuk, "that Cairo has twelve governors, of which two are the principal. The town is divided into twelve quarters, as Florence is into four; each emir governs his particular quarter and for his purpose has a large number of armed men."

Frescobaldi described the manner in which the women were veiled: "They are veiled in such a way that you can only see their eyes; the most distinguished women cover even their eyes with a transparent cloth through which they can see without being seen." The men wore white turbans and white clothes which could be of silk, cotton, or linen. They never wore boots, always a kind of slipper.

The city in whose houses people lived—except for a horde of the homeless who slept in the streets or in ruined buildings—had changed physically since Fatimid times. The most spectacular change was the work of the Nile. Its bed had moved steadily toward the west; its agglutinative silt had formed two important new islands, which in turn had become attached to the eastern bank.

The first was Bulak, which appeared as an island around the beginning of the fifteenth century, when Maqrizi, who tells of it, was probably living in the mausoleum of Barkuk. It was then joined by a causeway to the old bank near Maks. The causeway soon became solid earth. The attached island grew. As Maks had replaced the silted-up port of Fustat, so Bulak replaced Maks. Maks itself became silted up in the expansion of the east bank. By the end of the fourteenth century the hinterland of Bulak had become so large and so developed that a new canal, the

124

Khalig al-Nasri, was dug to bring water to plantations and farms.

A little to the northeast, a ship called the *Elephant* had been wrecked in late Fatimid times. Never salvaged, its skeleton attracted silt, sand, and debris which formed the nucleus of an island. By Saladin's time this second new island was under cultivation; by Kilawun's its revenues were considerable enough for the sultan to direct them to the upkeep of his college and hospital. By the end of the fourteenth century the island merged with Bulak and became an outlying agricultural suburb. The city of Cairo was now a considerable walk, or even donkey ride, from its source of fresh water and main artery to the outside world.

11

Mameluke Twilight

THE END OF A DYNASTY, from a distant viewpoint, seems inevitable and fast. To those living through the years concerned the result is hazardous; the doomed seems at moments likely to survive.

The reign of the last effective sultan is easily summarized. Kansuh al-Ghuri was the forty-sixth mameluke sultan and the twentieth of the Citadel Mamelukes. A contemporary of Caesar Borgia and the young Henry VIII, he reigned from 1501 to 1516. Starting life as a page to Qait Bey, he rose by slow degrees. He was over forty when made an emir of ten. By the time he came to the throne at sixty he had governed Tarsus, Aleppo, and Malatya. His reign was three times longer than average; his sins were less than those of many; his greed and need for money made him unpopular; he left behind an elegant mosque and college which still stand;[1] he died in battle resisting the Ottoman Turks. He was not to occupy his tomb. He left an adopted son who reigned but a few months.

But rather than abstract the sixteen years which reduced Cairo from the capital of an empire to a city bolting its doors at a new conqueror's approach, it is possible to slow time down and see, through the details of daily life and recurring incident, the texture of human existence in this twilit reign.

The details and incidents have been recorded. At least since the foundation of al-Azhar University, Cairo had been a highly literate city. Its citizens chronicled from the sidelines events they did not shape. For the mameluke twilight we have the journal of an Egyptian middle-class man. The accurate and careful record of Ibn Iyas,[2] brings alive the themes of those fatal days.

At the start of the sixteenth century the routine of Cairo life had a time-hallowed tone. The jostling for power between mameluke factions continued as it had done for two and a half centuries. This time it resulted in the election of Kansuh al-Ghuri. Since the death of Qait Bey in 1495, five sultans, debauched or incompetent, had squandered five years of wasteful interregnum.

Power was conferred in ceremonies which seemed destined to continue forever. Ibn Iyas writes:

> The enthronement of Kansuh al-Ghuri could be legalized by the caliph as soon as the Shafiyite and Hanifite cadis had arrived. They brought the new sultan the emblems of sovereignty: the black cloak and turban in which, despite his expressed forebodings, they now arrayed him. They gave him as his official titles 'al-Malik al-Ashraf' [The Most Noble King] and 'Abul-Nasr' [Father of Victory]. The whole of Cairo was lit up like a halo. He mounted the parade horse with its gilded saddle and saddle cloth by the stairway near the Gate of the Chain. Qait Rajabi stepped forward with the parasol and the Bird, the latter the symbol of his marshalhood. The caliph rode to the right of the sultan, while the chief officers processed before him in their most splendid robes. The procession having entered the royal palace through the Secret Door, the sultan seated himself upon the throne about twenty-five degrees before sunset, Cancer being in the ascendant. The first to kiss the ground before the new ruler was Qait Rajabi, followed by the other officers who filed past one by one. The sultan gave the caliph a robe of honor, who then returned to his house. The new sultan at this time was sixty. His beard showed not one white hair. This was considered an auspicious omen.

The sultan now took his place at the apex of the pyramid of state. Ibn Iyas starts each year in his journal with Muharram, the first month in the Arabic calendar. This calendar, based on the moon, progresses through the seasons of the solar year. Such occasions as Ramadan and the pilgrimage thus occur in steady rhythm through heat to cold then back again to heat. For example: "On Wednesday the 1st of Muharram the caliph Mutawakkil and the four cadis went to present their new year wishes to the sultan. It was a day of torrential rain, of hail and storm." The year in question[3] started in early March. A similar ceremony marked the beginning of each month: "On Thursday the 1st the sultan received the caliph and the four cadis in the pavilion of the Royal court, come to present their monthly felicitations."

The sultan presided at every kind of public occasion.

The chief religious occasion, as it had been for more than eight centuries, was the departure of the pilgrimage to Mecca.

> On 9 Rajab Cairo was decked with flags for the procession of the *mahmal*. The lancers wore their traditional red robes. Their chief was Timur Hasani, and the four supervisors were the same as the preceding year, but that the place of Abu Yazid, who had recently died, was taken by Misir Bey, the emir of kettledrums. The lancers performed their maneuvers better than the previous year. The sultan passed the night at the royal palace where he presided at a magnificent fireworks display. The mounted processions passed through the city streets in the ancient manner and the lancers processed twice in Meydan Rumeila. At the end of the parade, they dismounted and kissed the ground before the sultan, as had been done in the reign of Zahir Khoshkadam.[4] It is stated that Qait Bey introduced this new custom when he directed the *mahmal* procession. Then the *mahmal* was paraded, followed by the holy covering for the Kaaba and the tomb of Abraham. At the end of the ceremony the master of arms and the four supervisors went home, each gratified with a robe of honor.

Only three years before twilight darkened there seemed no reason why things might not continue as they had done for centuries. "This had been," Ibn Iyas sums up 1514, "a good year for the whole population, who lived in peace and happiness. There was abundance of cereals, amplitude of crops, particularly of

128

fruits such as melons. The Nile was high . . . ." That year the pilgrims had traveled back from Mecca in a record eleven days, with no mischance from disease or robbers. The month of pilgrimage had coincided with February. Things were usually more supportable for the pilgrims when their sacred journey took place in winter.

If the pilgrimage remained the focus of the religious year, the focus of the secular year was the rising of the Nile. So important was this material fact that it too was linked with religion. For example, on August 7, 1510:

> The sultan heard an entire reading of the Koran at the Nilometer, followed by a sumptuous banquet attended by the cadis and other notables. This ceremony took place because the Nile was rising very slowly. It was the 16th of the Coptic Mesori and the flood had not reached its height. Following the prayers of these important men the Nile rose that very night five fingers and fifteen the night following. The Nile continued to rise and reached its maximum height on 20 Mesori. The Canal was opened on the 21st, a week later than the preceding year.

When things went well or ill, the sultan was the center of public spectacle. He did not reign in remote seclusion from his subjects. In the spring of 1514 he returned from an emergency visit to Suez:

> On Saturday the 12th the sultan mounted his horse to traverse in solemn procession the city of Cairo, which he entered by the Gate of Victory. Preceded by his son, Nasir al-Din Muhammad, the sultan was in half dress, uncoiffed but for a simple royal skullcap, unaccompanied by royal standard, parasol or Bird. The four cadis, the emirs of a thousand who remained in Cairo, as well as civil functionaries, all took part in the procession. The sultan had given some of the officers who accompanied him pelisses, some of red velvet trimmed with sable, others of wool similarly trimmed. The people stood in front of their shops to watch the ruler pass. In the procession itself the sultan was preceded by two drums, two oboes and the long royal trumpets. Then came lines of dromedaries, four of which were

decked in pompons brocaded with gold, the others with pompons of velvet.

Ibn Iyas had a sharp ear for minor as well as important gossip. His comment on the death of the sultan's muezzin—whose voice had remarkable carrying power—is worthy of Pepys: "This was a man of outstanding morality. He died over forty, perhaps over fifty. It was reported of him that his insatiable sexual appetite was unsupportable to women. Nonetheless he had married a hundred times."

An amorous scandal, involving religious dignitaries, preoccupied public opinion to the exclusion of politics. It also involved the law of Islam, which was above the sultan as above everyone else.

An assistant to the Hanifite cadi had a beautiful wife whom Nureddin Mashali, assistant to the Shafiyite cadi, hopelessly loved. For a long time Mashali had tried to arrange an assignation. His chance came when the husband was to pass a night of prayer at a holy man's tomb. The wife at once informed her admirer who rushed round to her house, his delight untinged with fear. Unluckily, a neighbor, also attracted by this woman's beauty and aware of his rival's passion, watched for Mashali's coming and then hastened to interrupt the husband at his prayers. Returning home, the assistant to the Hanifite cadi found Mashali in his wife's bed. In vain the adulterer offered a thousand-dinar bribe; in vain the wife offered her husband the house and its contents. (In Islamic custom, these belonged to her, and would have been retained by her in the event of a divorce.) The stern cuckold insisted that the religious law (of which all the males in the story were exponents) should be applied. In his panic at being caught red-handed, Mashali was stupid enough to confess his crime before the chamberlain, who had him stripped naked and flogged almost to death. It was next the wife's turn. Supported on the shoulders of a burly warder, she received the same chastisement. The lovers' torments were only beginning. After pain, humiliation: perched on donkeys, their faces to the tails, they were paraded along Sharia Saliba and then through the lanes of the city before being returned to the chamberlain's house. After pain and humiliation, a fine: the chamberlain demanded a hundred dinars on his own account.

"But my husband had taken all I have," wailed the erring wife. "I have nothing to call my own."

Her husband, on refusing to hand over this sum, was also arrested. His son by another wife now carried the scandal one stage further. The boy was studying the Koran with members of the royal household. Hearing that his father was in prison, he rushed to the sultan and told him the story.

Al-Ghuri was anxious that his reign should be remembered for its strict enforcement of Koranic rules. He summoned the four cadis.

"You who are the chief magistrates of our faith," he said bitingly, "have indeed reasons to be proud. Some of your assistants drink wine; others commit adultery; others rob the pious endowments intended for the poor."

The sultan produced the affidavits relating to the affair. They carried the signature of the Shafiyite cadi who had recommended that the guilty pair should be stoned. The sultan insisted that the sentence (which had gone out of use early in Islamic times) should be applied. A trench was thereupon prepared for the man and woman; they would be forced to lie down in it while people stoned them.

If the sultan had not been busy with the departure of the pilgrims, this would have been the painful end of the affair. But the execution was briefly postponed.

This encouraged a brave man, Shams al-Din Zankaluni, to defend Mashali's case. Zankaluni, one of the assistants of the chief Shafiyite cadi, circulated the jurists with a paper in which he posed this case of conscience: "If a man admits to the sin of adultery, then goes back on his admission, should the penalty be maintained or quashed?"

Most of the jurists agreed that in such a case the penalty of stoning should be lifted, and no punishment should be inflicted at all.

The sultan raged at a verdict typical of the practical tolerance of Islam. For though Islamic penalties for adultery were harsh, harsher still were the precautions against the penalties being enforced without overwhelming evidence to support the charge. For adultery to be proved there had to be either open confession, or the testimony of five witnesses. One outraged husband was not enough.

Al-Ghuri told them to stop splitting hairs. "A man steals to his neighbor's house, is discovered between his neighbor's coverlets, confesses his crime, and signs the affidavit. And now you would claim that his confession can be withdrawn?"

The sultan convened a new Council which included many other jurists besides the cadis and put the question afresh. Quoting traditional sayings of the Prophet, a jurist reiterated that the law of God protected the man. When the sultan retorted that he alone was responsible and would decide, the jurist replied:

"Without doubt you are responsible, but inside the context of the Holy Law. If you sentence this couple to death, you will have to pay the price of blood." He was supported by the consensus of the Council.

Foaming with rage at what he took to be casuistry, the sultan dismissed the jurists. One was promptly removed from his post of intendant of the sultan's college; another lost his honorific position as preacher in the sultan's mosque. Al-Ghuri's greatest rage was reserved for the jurist who had originally proposed stoning and then gone back on his own proposal. From being an intimate adviser to the sultan, he was now thrown into cold disfavor. The adulterer and his accomplice were thrown into dungeons. As for the brave Zankaluni, he was brought before the sultan in the hippodrome with his two children. The father was stretched on the ground and given a thousand stripes; each of his sons received six hundred. Streaming blood, they were then mounted on donkeys. By the month's end Zankaluni was reported dead.

In a frenzy of puritan zeal (and still meditating how to punish the guilty couple), the sultan turned his wrath on drunken schoolmasters. For each tipsy pedagogue arrested he promised the prefect of Cairo a separate robe.

A week later a scaffold was erected outside the house of one of the jurists. As the sultan had hoped, the man's household were convinced that the jurist's last hour had come. They began to lament. But it was Mashali and his mistress who were brought to the place and hanged, according to the sultan's orders, face to face on a single rope. For two days their corpses dangled outside the house. Meanwhile four new cadis were appointed to replace the old.

132

Besides illustrating the narrow limits within which freedom moved, this story illustrates that courage could grow from unfriendly soil. Zankaluni's name deserves remembrance.

Al-Ghuri's love of justice had its limits. Ibn Iyas, though interested in spectacle and scandal, does not deprive his tapestry of the somber threads of truth. He quotes two opposite sentences in one month of 1506. A poor dervish from Upper Egypt is dragged before the sultan, accused of "atheism, sorcery, and the use of milk for his ablutions and intimate toilet." His transgressions of Islamic law are rewarded as follows: he is paraded naked through the streets on the back of a camel, then hanged under the windows of a college. A little later a sheikh who professes mysticism and practices coining is arrested with his counterfeiting tools. The sultan sentences him to lose both hands. But because he is a former mameluke and has powerful military friends, the sentence is canceled and he is retired in some haste to Jerusalem.

The sultan's forebodings at the moment of his election had not been a pose. He had lived amidst the machinery of state all his life. He foresaw that his sultanate would have four powerful enemies: the Bedouin, the resurgent nations of western Europe, the Ottoman Turks, and his own mamelukes.

Cairo was nominally the capital of an empire which included, in addition to Egypt, western Arabia, Palestine, Syria, and parts of southern Anatolia. Throughout these far-flung domains nomads challenged the mameluke power. Inside Egypt itself the revenues of whole provinces were at the mercy of armed Bedouin raids; Fayum in particular was under constant attack. Mecca, a prized possession of the mameluke state, was besieged; the lawless Bedouin with their superficial faith and their profound contempt for settled peoples regarded the pilgrims as their legitimate prey. "On Wednesday the 26th, the postman of the pilgrimage reached Cairo after a considerable delay. There had been a Bedouin attack. They had stripped him of everything, including his horse and all the letters sent by the pilgrims, so that this year their relatives received no news of them. The postman had walked on foot for two days, dressed only in a strip of cloth. The sultan and the people alike were distressed by this pitiful news."

The Bedouin were exploiting the growing impudence of the sultan's other foes. Having driven the Franks from Palestine, the mamelukes had controlled for centuries the trade routes to the East. This control accounted for much of Egypt's wealth. Now the Franks had learned to sail round the Cape of Good Hope; Vasco da Gama's feat had initiated regular voyages by Portuguese ships to the Indian Ocean. Inside the mameluke empire suspicion of Franks was widespread. In summer 1510: "News came from Mecca that the Sherif Barakat, lord of the city, had arrested three Europeans disguised in the clothes of Asia Minor. Their European identity was proved by the fact they were uncircumcised. Considered as spies for some European prince, they were put in irons and sent to the sultan."

By March 1514 there were severe shortages of food. No ship had put into Alexandria for a whole year. "No ships had reached Jedda either, because of the European pirates who sailed the Indian Ocean. In fact, it was now six years since merchandise had been unloaded at the port of Jedda." The sultan prepared a fleet at Suez to drive these pirates away. Detachments of mamelukes were prepared for intervention as far afield as India.

Inevitability, one repeats, is discerned after the sequence of events has unrolled. At the time, recovery, reconquest, reversal of defeat, still seem possible.

But in this struggle between Europeans and the sons of Islam, the latter were divided. Two new Muslim powers ruled to the north and to the east of the mameluke domains: a Sufi dynasty, the Safawids, ruled Persia and Iraq, while the growing Ottoman empire ruled western Asia Minor and much of the Balkans.

The Ottomans had been slowly consolidating their half-European, half-Asian state for several centuries. After the setback of the Mongol invasions, they had recovered and gone on to conquer, in the name of orthodox Islam, the 'new Rome' on the Bosphorus which had embodied the Christian antagonist to twenty-five generations of Muslims. Their ambition seemed insatiable.

In July 1512 Ibn Iyas notes what at first seems an ordinary start to a month:

> The caliph and the four cadis went up to present their monthly felicitations to the sultan. The same day an

134

ambassador from the prince of Tunis presented a magnificent present to the sultan. Its value was put at ten thousand dinars. It consisted of precious stuffs, horses, arms, and other objects of value. Before leaving the Citadel, he received a woolen cloak trimmed with sable. He was followed by an Ottoman ambassador, who carried a message to the sultan. It was rumored that the Ottoman ruler Bayazid was about to die and had abdicated in favor of Selim, his son, who would now rule Asia Minor.

Collision between Selim and al-Ghuri did not seem inevitable. The sultan in Constantinople and the sultan in Cairo supported one and the same religion. Both powers had, in the growing strength of Europe, a common foe. Ordinary people in Cairo probably assumed that all was still well when in 1514 another Ottoman ambassador arrived. "The Ottoman ambassador made his official call, introduced by Azdamur, the chief of protocol, and accompanied by several officers of the guard. He brought with him a sumptuous present: twenty-five loads of lynx, sable, and ermine, of Bursa velvet, of colored fabrics from Samarkand, of silver vases, to say nothing of twenty-five young mamelukes of outstanding beauty." In return al-Ghuri invited the ambassador to a Nilometer evening; a feast was embellished by the voices of the best reciters of the Koran.

Euphoria would last to within months of the final clash.

Behind the exchange of gifts lay Selim's primary obsession: a detestation of those forms of Islam which were mystical or Shiite in tendency. Selim had already massacred 40,000 of his own Anatolian subjects whom he regarded as heretical. He was now preparing a punitive war against Shiite Persia. The purport of the embassies was clear: al-Ghuri must choose to be the ally of Selim, or his foe. The issue was complicated because of al-Ghuri's links with certain statelets on the borders between Selim's empire and that of the Persian Shah. If they became involved in an Ottoman–Persian clash, al-Ghuri would be in trouble. Ibn Iyas knew what was going on. "Deeply worried by the conflict between the Ottomans and the Persians, the sultan visited the tombs of the Imam Shafiy and the Imam Laith; that day he distributed largesse to the poor." Although al-Ghuri disliked Sufism as much as did Selim, he feared that the collision between his two great Muslim neighbors would soon involve Egypt. Selim was ambitious as well as bigoted. Nor can he have been pleased by the experience on mameluke territory of one of his ambassadors. "In the course of the night they stole from under his very pillow the valise in which he kept his linen and money, as well as the letter from the Ottoman sovereign. The sultan tore his beard and threatened the Arab sheikh of the area concerned that if he did not return the ambassador's belongings by nightfall, he would personally cut him to pieces fully dressed." Happily the valise was found.

But throughout al-Ghuri's reign, up to the moment when the Ottomans attacked mameluke territory in northern Syria, his great preoccupation—and Cairo's nearest danger—lay in the mamelukes themselves. When war came, one venal mameluke betrayed his caste; the other mamelukes did little to prevent their own defeat.

The irresponsible violence of these virilistic louts runs like an anarchic thread through the pages of Ibn Iyas. No one is safe from their rage when their payment is less than they think their due. If meat is short, they demonstrate. Their horses charge through the narrow lanes of the city; the terrified shopkeepers rush to close the iron-studded doors which separate the quarters. Unexplained crimes are laid to their account. Often they kill their own. "The sultan's mameluke Barsbay Hudaya was killed this month. A former mameluke of Zahir Khoshkadam, he was found at home with his throat cut; with him similarly murdered was one of his slaves. Though no killers were identified, it was assumed they were mameluke recruits anxious to steal Hudaya's gratuity. His way of life was in any case deplorable."

Mameluke riots were like revolts. More than once the aging sultan offered to resign if the slaves could choose someone they liked better than himself.

One account of a mameluke disturbance may suffice for all.

In the early autumn of 1515, the tutor to the royal children, Sunbul, a respected and wealthy black eunuch, had overheard a young mameluke using filthy language. The schoolmaster had the ruffian bastinadoed on his feet. Unfortunately for Sunbul, the mameluke had taken to his bed and died. The mamelukes prepared for revolt. Besieging the entrance to the Citadel, they drove off the duty officer in panic. They then sacked the shops in a wasteland near the Citadel known as the Tartar Ruins. Next, they decided, they would loot the city markets. The threat of continuing violence forced the sultan to negotiate. The angry mamelukes presented him with a stiff ultimatum:

> Either you hand Sunbul over to us, or you pay each of us a hundred dinars. More, we insist on respect. Shop-keepers have taken to seizing the bridles of our horses and heaping us with abuse. Since your reign began, we mamelukes are no longer respected by the people.

Rather than disburse, al-Ghuri preferred to surrender Sunbul. The poor wretch, in a torn white robe and simple skullcap, his bloodshot eyes blinking in the sunlight, was led staggering from his dungeon. The waiting mamelukes set upon him, eager to use their sabers there and then. In vain he pleaded that they accept a thousand dinars as an indemnity for their dead friend. They dragged him down to the water trough at the foot of the stair-case and there sawed him in two. Ibn Iyas comments that this was the first time a eunuch had suffered this particular fate.

After such disturbances, the sultan and his officer would im-pose a curfew on all mamelukes, valets, reservists, and Negro slaves. The carrying of arms would be forbidden. Mamelukes would be prohibited from molesting the keepers of stalls or from veiling their faces. For a moment the people would rejoice and go about their business—until the next excuse for the next distur-bance.

When a challenger to this system appeared on the Syrian horizon, the people of Cairo were panicky spectators. Though an amnesty was offered to thieves and cutthroats who would turn their talents against the Turks, no one thought of organizing the ordinary Egyptians to defend their homes.

The tired al-Ghuri, a pot-bellied man of seventy-eight, devoted to plants and flowers, his round little beard still nearly black, his gnarled fingers loaded with enormous rings, prepared to meet Selim in northern Syria. The mameluke troops, after hag-gling over their pay, departed with the usual fanfares. The pro-cession of troops and dignitaries entered Cairo from the south, through Bab Zuweyla, and traversed the ancient road 'Between the Two Palaces' to issue at Bab al-Nasr, where they camped for their last night. On their way through the city the distinctive joy-cries of Egyptian women—made by holding one hand under the nose and waggling the tongue in mid-scream—had followed them from the rooftops. It was a splendid scene. The caliph was twenty yards in advance of the sultan; he wore, we are told, a turban of the Baghdad style, its two ends hanging down; his Baalbek tunic had a silken border.

The mameluke army, swollen with a retinue of muezzins, learned men and musicians, followed the coast road through Palestine. Syrian and Bedouin contingents joined it as it advanced. Al-Ghuri rode in triumph through the streets of a carpeted Damascus; European merchants scattered gold to the crowd.

In September news filtered back to Egypt of a disaster without remembered parallel. Khairbey, the mameluke governor in Aleppo, had made a deal with the Ottomans; his deliberate bad advice and treachery in battle destroyed the Egyptians. The sultan and his royal mamelukes fought bravely but in vain against an Ottoman army superior in numbers and guns. Al-Ghuri was slain and his head sent to Selim.

The last act of mameluke sovereignty is a compound of the gallantry which had often distinguished individual sultans and the collective irresponsibility of a system which in no sense relied on the majority of its subjects. While the Ottomans consolidated their hold on Syria and prepared to advance south, the Cairenes spread rumors. These were alarming: the Turks had beheaded hundreds of mamelukes in Aleppo; they had drunk alcohol, smoked hashish, and raped little boys in holy Ramadan. As for the mamelukes, they took a month to decide whom to elect as sultan. The fatal honor fell on al-Ghuri's adoptive son, Tumanbey. He had passed the usual ladder. A boy slave presented to Qait Bey, he had then been freed, given a uniform and horse, made page of the wardrobe, promoted in his thirties to Secretary of State. He was as reluctant as al-Ghuri to don the dangerous black robe and turban, to assume the Bedouin sword. (Those other emblems of the sultanate, the parasol and Bird, could not be found in the quartermaster's stores.) Tumanbey doubted if his treasury could afford the usual accession donation to the mamelukes. (A desire for such a donation was one reason why short sultanates were liked.)

Tumanbey's reign was short indeed. Yet even in his three months of power the old order continued to function as before:

solemn processions, dignified prayers, such spectacles as the sultan's wife reaching the Citadel at the moment of morning prayer, by the light of lanterns and torches, escorted by a throng of princesses and ladies of high society, by the wives of officers and dignitaries of state.

But the rapid Ottoman seizure of the Levant could not be disguised. This year the *mahmal* could not leave for Mecca; the woven covering for the Kaaba had to be smuggled out. Yet even now there were rumors of hope. The Bedouin would finish off the Turks; the Turks would catch the plague; Syria would prove a grave for the Ottoman army.

Selim's first communication with Tumanbey was grim: "From the part of Our Majesty whom fate has favored, to the emir Tumanbey: God has revealed to me that I shall take over the world, that I shall master all its regions, from east to west, as was done before by Alexander of the Two Horns." Selim went on to argue that while Tumanbey was a slave, he himself was a prince, twentieth in a line of princes, and had secured the Egyptian sultanate by the death of al-Ghuri. Selim offered Tumanbey the chance of being his vassal. Let him be responsible for sending tribute to Constantinople, as it had once been sent to Baghdad, and all would be well. Selim would confirm the emir as his viceroy. Otherwise he could occupy Egypt and behead every Circassian to be found.

Even as the sword of Damocles hung over them on fraying string, the mamelukes could not concentrate their thoughts. They rejected Tumanbey's sensible suggestion that they come to terms with Selim. He next suggested that they should fight without pay: "You are about to defend your existence, and that of your wives and children. There's not a dinar nor a dirham left in the Treasury. I am your equal. I shall share your fate. But I have nothing to offer you in cash."

The sincerity of the sultan—whose character seems nobler than any in the long annals of his caste—fired some of the young recruits. They would fight to avenge al-Ghuri, their patron. The hardened veterans were canny. "We won't move unless you give each of us 130 dinars." A desperate officer suggested a levy on the goods of orphans, on the pious endowments—anything to get the mamelukes their cash. The sultan refused. "Such arbitrary measures will never disgrace my reign."

This undignified haggling delayed the departure of a force which might have held Gaza. Now it was too late. Tumanbey's plan to meet the Ottomans at the edge of the desert, when they would be fatigued by their trek, was turned down. The decisive battle was fought on the plain near Mattaria, within sight of the obelisk of Amen-Re.

Despite the sultan's bravery—with a band of faithful followers he fought his way to Selim's war tent—the mamelukes were routed; the Ottomans had sent a force over the Mokattam hills which took them in the rear. While Tumanbey escaped to organize Bedouin resistance, the Ottomans occupied Cairo and massacred every Circassian they could find.

Selim was impressed by Tumanbey. The mameluke sultan refused to surrender. For one night he even succeeded in recapturing Cairo, until the Ottoman army counterattacked from its camp at Bulak. Selim was statesman enough to see that so brave a man would make a better governor than Khairbey, who, having betrayed once, might well betray again. He would send an embassy to Tumanbey, whose success in rousing Upper Egypt against the Ottomans had surprised everyone. He instructed the caliph (who had adjusted his prayers and felicitations to a new master) to lead a party of Ottoman officials and the four cadis. The caliph, embarrassed, sent his deputy instead. The delegation was empowered to offer Tumanbey Egypt as his fief. Once again the mamelukes betrayed their leader. To force his hand against such a solution they summarily murdered the Ottoman ambassadors as well as one of the cadis who was thought to be against the mamelukes.

A last two-day battle between Tumanbey's force of Bedouin and mamelukes was fought near the pyramids. Once again Ottoman arms prevailed against ferocious courage. Tumanbey took refuge with a Bedouin sheikh whose life he had once saved. The sheikh sold him to the Turks and the last mameluke sultan was led in chains before Selim. Tumanbey spoke so nobly, defended himself so passionately, that even now Selim considered a pardon. Khairbey, the traitor of Aleppo, turned the scales, whispering to Selim that only the death of Tumanbey could make Egypt safe.

From the Ottoman camp at Bulak, preceded by 400 Ottoman soldiers, the last sultan was led through Maks to Cairo, returning the salutes of the crowd who had only recently cheered Selim. No one had told him where he was being taken or why. When the cortege halted at Bab Zuweyla, the normal place of execution, when Ottoman officers surrounded him with drawn sabers, Tumanbey knew his fate. He shouted to the crowd to join him in a triple recitation of the Opening Prayer of the Koran. Three times the vast crowd chanted the sacred words "*Bismillah al-rahman al-raheem* . . . ." In the name of God, the Merciful, the Compassionate.

"Now, hangman, do your work."

So, bare-headed, the handsome sultan was hanged like any slave. It was a bungled job. The rope broke twice before Tumanbey was choked to death.

12

Mameluke Night

THE CAIRO TOWNSFOLK HAD PITIED the fate of Tumanbey; they had admired his qualities; but they had suffered too long from the mamelukes as a whole to believe that one virtuous sultan could transform the system. Hoping perhaps for a new Saladin, they examined their conqueror as he paraded through Cairo. Preceded by his infantry and cavalry, Selim entered by Bab al-Nasr in the north and traversed the immemorial axis of the city to issue at Bab Zuweyla on the return road to his camp at Bulak. The women making their traditional joy-cries saw a bent little man of forty dressed in an unpretentious turban and a velvet kaftan. His eyes and nose were large, his complexion an ashen gray, and his chin clean-shaven. He looked unpleasant and ill at ease.

Public sympathy soon turned against Selim. The systematic slaughter of the Circassians outraged a people whose own rages never lasted long. Even mosques provided no sanctuary. Apart from the many killed 'resisting arrest,' no fewer than 800 mamelukes were said to have been beheaded in front of Selim. The executioner sorted the heads as he cut them off, Circassians in one pile, servants and slaves in another. The mameluke heads were then strung on ropes for display in the Middle Island (the future Gezira). The bodies were flung into the Nile.

Despite such diversions, it is doubtful if Selim enjoyed his half year in Cairo. He prayed in several mosques; he made trite comments on the pyramids; he visited the public bath of Khoshkadam, then another in Bulak where, according to Ibn Iyas, "he gave twenty dinars to the *hammam* boy, whose service had pleased him." He had a mishap at the Nilometer. His favorite ring, an early Ottoman heirloom, was a massive affair of silver worked with astrological devices of the utmost import. This ring fell into the Nile and despite the efforts of many divers was not recovered. Eager for the cooler climate of the Bosphorus, Selim embarked from near the Nilometer on May 29, 1517, for the down-river journey to the Mediterranean. With him from Alexandria sailed many of the treasures of Cairo, from the Citadel and the mosques. No fewer than eighteen hundred Egyptian workmen and artists were instructed to leave for the new imperial capital. Also ordered to Constantinople was Mutawakkil, the last Abbasid caliph. In Constantinople the caliph was at first well treated. But his scandalous morals afforded Selim a pretext to jail him. Released by Selim's successor, Suliman the Magnificent, he was paid a pension of sixty dirhams. When he finally resigned his office and all claims to caliphal status, he was permitted to retire to Cairo, where he died in 1538. Neither Selim nor Suliman claimed the caliphal title for themselves. For one thing, they did not belong to the Prophet's tribe of Qoreysh; for another, they relied on their army and administration, not on empty titles. Only much later, as Ottoman power declined, was the notion of an Ottoman caliphate advanced. The institution, a feeble crutch for failing fortunes, was finally abolished by Kemal Ataturk in 1924.

Because of the Ottomans, Cairo had lost in one year its sultan and caliph, its independence in politics and in religion. This spectacular downgrading was a grievous blow to the pride of its citizens, though in a sense they were merely exchanging one form of foreign rule for another.

Because of the Europeans Cairo lost something more ultimately vital: its strategic and economic importance. The Europeans, unlike the Ottomans, were invisible on the immediate skyline; their effect was nonetheless far-reaching. In May, 1498, in the same decade which had seen Columbus discover America, Vasco da Gama had sailed into the port of Calicut on the southwest coast of India. Even al-Ghuri, preoccupied as he had been with his mamelukes and Bedouin at home, with the Ottomans abroad, had recognized the threat: hence his frequent visits to Suez and his attempts to build up a fleet to drive the Europeans from the Indian Ocean. Vasco da Gama's circumnavigation of Africa was no mere feat of sailing. It symbolized Europe's escape from her virtual imprisonment in the cold and isolated north. Except for the Venetians, who controlled Europe's trade with the Middle East, the Franks had been barred from trading with India and China by the barrier of the mameluke state. This barrier had prevented pepper, a commodity which in that age ranked with precious stones, from being freely imported into Europe. Egypt, as middleman, raised by three hundred per cent the prices for pepper and the other spices which had become more and more valued in European kitchens. By turning this barrier and breaking this Islamic monopoly (which the new Ottoman masters of Egypt were not able to reimpose) the Europeans reduced the value of Egypt as an addition to the Ottoman empire. Ottoman interest in the province was, as a result, to flag.

But although Cairo lost its independence and its chief source of revenue, it did not lose its mamelukes. Despite the deaths in battle of those who had fought to the end, despite the massacres, many thousands survived. Selim found it more convenient to use the mamelukes than to destroy them. Since the Ottoman interest had traditionally been in southeastern Europe and since Egypt was no longer of key strategic and commercial importance, he decided to concentrate on expanding his empire in the Balkans and to regard Egypt as a source of tribute. Its agriculture remained considerable. The mamelukes, having no bonds of sympathy with the Egyptians, were ideal tribute-collectors. Selim is reported to have punished with death a vizir who suggested the confiscation of the mameluke estates. Instead he used the mamelukes as one element in a complicated system designed to get as much from Egypt as possible, while discouraging any moves toward independence. A pasha ruled from the citadel with the backing of five thousand janissaries, the crack Ottoman soldiers recruited as a boy levy from the Balkan Christians. The pasha was advised by a divan of Ottoman officers and religious notables. At the same time the mameluke emirs were confirmed in their property and the twelve sanjaks into which Egypt was divided were each headed by an emir.

The reprieved mamelukes could no longer aspire to be sultans; but after the tribute was paid they could enjoy, as lordly beys, whatever they could extort from the Egyptians. There was less to extort than before. Egypt was no longer a sovereign country with trading ramifications throughout the world; as trade declined, the Bedouin became an increasing menace. But what of wealth remained—and it declined with the population which produced it—was theirs to share and enjoy. As Ottoman society weakened at its center, so the power of the chief mameluke—known as Sheikh al-Balad, or Lord of the Town—increased. The feuds between mameluke factions also increased.

But the city began to dwindle.

It was visited several times—his visits straddled the transition to Ottoman rule—by Leo Africanus. (The name Leo was given to the converted Moor by Pope Leo X, who had been godfather at his baptism.) Leo estimated the population of Cairo within its walls as not more than eight thousand families; that is, around 40,000 people. These were "noblemen, gentlemen and merchants that sell wares brought from all other places." The figure did not include Bulak, which under the Ottomans became increasingly important.

Some constants were unchanged. The focus of the year was still the Nile flood. The Nilometer was read and prices for food were fixed by the clerk of the market "according as he knoweth by the foresaid experiment that the high and low grounds of Egypt have received either too little or too much or convenient moisture: all which customs and ceremonies being duly performed, there followeth so great a solemnity, and such a thundering noise of drums and trumpets throughout all Cairo, that a man would suppose the whole city to be turned upside down. And then every family hath a barge adorned with rich coverings and carpets, and with torchlight, and furnished with the most dainty meats and confections, wherewith they solace themselves." At the breaking of the dam, "the river of Nilus is so swiftly and forcibly carried through that conduit and through all other conduits and sluices in the city and the suburbs, that Cairo at that time seemed to be another Venice; and then you may row over all the places of the land of Egypt."

The next century and a half isolated Egypt still further from the outside world. The citizens of Cairo knew nothing of that astonishing outburst of creativity which marked the rebirth of scientific discovery in western Europe. The Muslims had transmitted the Indian numerals (wrongly called Arabic) to the West; they had invented algebra and had continued the great medical tradition of the Greeks; they were unaware of the ways in which these legacies were being exploited by their western heirs. Complacent in an unchanging faith, they were indifferent to the spiritual questioning which had begun in the Reformation and continued through the philosophic movements of the seventeenth and eighteenth centuries. The colonization of the Americas, the new trading contacts between Europe and the Far East, the development of printing, all these were distant rumors to a country suffering, behind its provincial barricades, from pointless violence; clashes between the pasha's soldiers and the mamelukes, between the Bedouin and settled authority, between the arrogant beys themselves. Famine and pestilence were constants as they had always been. In the spring of 1619, to cite one instance only, plague killed no fewer than 635,000 persons.

To the outside world Egypt had become almost a land of Prester John. Anything could be related of it, little was sure. In 1670 John Ogilby published a vast tome on Africa which he had compiled from his reading of ancient experts and recent travelers. In the section devoted to Egypt engraved plates showed such wonders as a great-breasted female sphinx (much like the head and shoulders of a well-barbered Restoration lady) rising from the sand amidst thickets of pyramids so sharply angled they resembled spikes. Ogilby entirely accepted the truth of three-thousand-year-old lamps found still burning "in the caves under Memphis." Only when he used reason or the Bible could he rebut absurdity. For example, he refuted Prince Radzovil's suggestion that the Jews had built the pyramids: "With how little reason it may be imagined that the Israelites should build these pyramids may appear, in that they are built of stone, whereas their employment was all in brick-work."

Ogilby has a fair notion of those aspects of Cairo which the occasional merchant still reported. "The principal inhabitants are Moors,[2] Turks, Jews, Copts, Grecians and Armenians. At this day it is the prime of all the Egyptian cities, exceeding in bigness Rome, Constantinople and most others by us accounted the greatest, being in circuit, according to Villamont, two and twenty leagues, so that a horseman in full speed can scarce ride about it in ten hours."

A stranger would enter Cairo by way of Bulak, now the main area of commerce as well as the port. The island of Bulak was now firmly part of the east bank; a substantial Ottoman mosque served the religious needs of a place where dwelt "artificers and tradesmen, especially such as deal in corn, oil and sugar." (We notice the absence of spices, now ferried direct to Europe.)

But Ogilby's description of the Bulak waterfront makes us feel we are in Atlantis—or in one of those schoolboy essays where the puzzled pupil invents as he goes along: "The stately churches and palaces fronting the Nile yield a pleasant and delightful prospect, although its beauty is much diminished and impaired by the several wars, in which it has had no mean share of suffering." Ogilby may be referring to mosques when he speaks of churches (as his contemporaries spoke of the Christian god as Jove). But we know that except for the Bulak mosque, the great shrines of Cairo avoided the waterfront, for the simple reason that it was so unstable, being liable to wholesale inundation at the time of flood. Nor had Cairo's dereliction come about through wars.

Ogilby introduces us to a name which is to become more and more prominent in the history of Cairo:

> From Bulak to Grand Cairo the land is all flat, and the way very pleasant, being much frequented with travellers; but the most beautiful part is a place called Usbechia in the suburbs, near the city-gate; this Usbechia is a round piece of land, encompassed about with houses, which yield a prospect infinitely pleasant, not only when the fields are decked with flowers, but also when by the recess of the Nile, it seems like a drained pond, full of various forms of living fishes.

The lake of Ezbekiah—named after Ezbek al-Tutush, a fifteenth-century emir—was filled each year with the Nile flood; around it the great mamelukes built their palaces. It was the smart area of a city whose statistics puzzled Ogilby. One of his sources made the fantastic statement that Cairo contained no less that 6,800 remarkable mosques, and in addition, 24,000 ordinary ones. How many houses? "The houses by some accounted 30,000, but with those in the suburbs, about Cairo, in Bulak and adjoining, are little less than 300,000. Each of them is on the top flat, as most of the houses in Egypt." The shape of Cairo is equally obscure:

> Villamont says the form of it is oval; but Belloon triangular, of which the castle lying upon a hill makes one angle, whence the walls are the second, and thence going to the north shapes the third, wherein is a fort and castle. And whereas both the city and suburbs are close built, with a great number of sumptuous and stately edifices, which hinder the sight of the walls, therefore such as have but superficially viewed it, have taken occasion to say that Cairo is without walls, whereas in truth it is encompassed with strong walls and gates, of which the last are all plated over, and strengthened with iron. . . .

Ogilby creates his Cairo rather as Shakespeare his Illyria. Like the flowers which enamel the fields near Ezbekiah (wild flowers are hardly a feature of the brief Egyptian spring), like the churches the waterfront, like the lamps in tombs, like the big-breasted sphinx, much is imagination composing a city less and less accessible to Western visitors. The following scene seems inspired by a puritan spirit: it is set at Bab al-Louk, first the silt land deposited by the Nile, then the polo ground of Aibek, and in the time of Bibars an area of villas.

> The common people hereof, after the Mahumetan Public *Sahala* [a creditable miss-shot for *salah*, meaning prayer] is ended, give themselves up to all lasciviousness and debaucheries, and seeing of vain sights, and idle shows, for out of the city stage-players, jugglers and morris-dancers present themselves, showing many camels, asses and dogs in a ridiculous manner dancing to make sport.

Vegetation partakes of the general mystery. Under the branches of the Virgin's tree no one born out of wedlock is able to pass. The balsam trees growing nearby—"they are high, with very few leaves which as Dioscorides saith, are of a green colour, whitish, and do not fall off in winter"—produce in summer *opobalsamum*.

"As soon as it cometh into the air it becomes whitish, afterwards green, then of a gold colour, lastly paler; the strained balsam is at first clear, but becomes instantly thick and cloudy, and when old, groweth like turpentine; when it first drops it is of so strong a smell, as causeth in many the head-ache, and in some causes a sudden bleeding at the nose." This balsam seems to have been the Tiger-Balm of the seventeenth century. The Egyptians "apply it almost against all diseases proceeding from cold, moisture or poison, curing with it all wounds that are not deep, and accompanied with fractured bones or cut sinews, in a short time. It heals also all venomous bitings of serpents and scorpions, either taken inwardly, or spread upon the wound. It is an extraordinary preservative against the plague, taking half a quarter of an ounce inwardly. It drives away all inveterate agues and fevers that proceed from putrification, cleanseth all unconcocted and cold humors and inward obstructions, if daily a quarter of an ounce be taken inwardly. Very operative in opening oppilations and concocting indigested and superfluous humors; it restores lost sight, and hearing, if it be dropped warm into either of the offended parts; it is a very powerful medicine against all cramps derived from cold and moisture; against the vertigo or dizziness of the head, the falling sickness, lameness, palsy, shaking of the limbs, cough, stoppings of the chest, consumption of the lungs, a weak stomach, difficulty of breathing, fits of the mother, stopping of the courses, the whites, stopping of the urine and the colic; the stone in the bladder and veins it powerfully breaks and dissipates."

Inaccuracy of detail cannot mar the charm of Ogilby's description of the chief constant of the religious year:

> From Cairo also set forth the Turkish pilgrims which annually travel in caravans to Mecca, to visit Mahomet's sepulchre. This is the head city of Arabia Felix lying by the Red Sea: eight days journey from which is Medina, where is Mahomet's tomb; to which out of Egypt once a year in November,[3] go sometimes twelve or fifteen, nay, sometimes forty-thousand pilgrims to offer according to their ability, sacrifice and burnt-offerings to their Prophet.[4] Over the whole caravan, one superior commander is appointed, called Hamirag,[5] who leads them under the conduct and safeguard of three hundred soldiers furnished with bows and muskets to

Mecca and Medina, and without much delay and hindrance brings them back to Cairo (except sometimes assaulted, hurt, plundered and slain by the Arabians in the wilderness). The number of camels attending this great company are accounted by some sixty, and by others ninety thousand. The Grand Seignior[6] alone bestows upon this pilgrimage, without accounting particular expenses of the people, six hundred thousand ducats, a fourth part of the whole revenue of Egypt; for many poor people and beggars go thither on foot without any money or provision, for whom the Grand Seignior causes many camels to be furnished, to be ready in case of sickness, faintness or weariness.

Each person must provide himself of all necessaries, even to water, because on the whole way there is scarce any to be found. Before the caravan sets forth, all the pilgrims and waggons are to be viewed and searched, which in good order passing quite through Cairo from the castle[7] where the pasha dwells, draw forth out of the city gates into an open field, where they wait for one another, and sometimes above eight days are spent before they are all gotten together.

Before the caravan march the troops of horse, or cavalcade, followed by the chief bakers, cooks, smiths, sutlers and other artificers, each having a camel laden with necessaries needful for their journey. Then follow the horses of the Hamirag, or superior commander, some of which carry vessels of water, others several necessary things to be used on the way. After these horses two camels, which are to draw waggons or chariots, accompained with a great number of other camels, some with burdens and some without, in time of need to carry the poor and those that are sick, as we mentioned before; after that a great number of other camels belonging to persons of quality, and many musketeers and pilgrims on foot, following the janissaries that are bravely set out with muskets and with plumes in their turbans; then the commander of the caravan and other volunteer votaries. Last of all, a small pavilion of silk stitched with gold, is carried upon a camel, by which he so becomes enfranchised and for ever after freed from bearing burdens, and honoured with a stately caparison thrown over him at the tomb of Mahomet.

Leo Africanus saw a Cairo whose sovereignty had but recently been withdrawn, when the effects of economic loss were but beginning; Ogilby wrote his composite portrait of a land of Prester John when the decline of the Ottoman empire had just begun; the shrewdest observer of all—the same Volney whose puzzlement at the mameluke system has been noted already—visited Egypt and the Levant between 1783 and 1785. He shrewdly observed mameluke society in its final decadence.

What impressed Volney first was the depopulation of Egypt and its capital. No more than in Ogilby's day were there accurate statistics. Guesses were various. A Baron le Toff had put the population of Cairo with Bulak (the port was still separated by open country from the town it served) at 700,000; in 1761 a M. Neibuhr had estimated that the city's periphery was comparable to that of Paris. Volney argued that while most houses in orderly Paris were five stories high, those in Cairo were generally of two stories, when they were not ruined, which in vast areas they were. He therefore estimated the city's population at a quarter of a million against the three-quarters of a million living in Paris. He put the population of Egypt at just over two million. His figures were probably almost right.

By eighteenth-century standards the city was an aesthetic mess; by any standard it was in physical disrepair: "Cairo lacks those public or private buildings, those regular squares, those aligned roads, which enable architecture to display its beauties. The outskirts are marked by dusty hills, formed by the daily accumulation of rubbish." The sense of sight and smell were alike affronted by the dirt and dereliction. Even more disgusting than the outward aspect—where the rich apparel of a few horsemen contrasted with the rags of the pedestrian many—was the inward aspect of mameluke rule. With increasing brutality the beys divided a diminishing wealth. "All that one sees and hears proclaims that one is in the land of slavery and tyranny." These were strong words from an admirer of Voltaire who had embarked from the France of Louis XVI.

The mameluke, in Volney's account, emerged as the most expensive soldier in history. Each Ramadan he expected a new suit of clothes. He required the best materials from France, Venice, Damascus, and India. He coveted jewels, pistols, Arabian steeds, and Kashmir shawls. His women had long since discarded the old use of sequins as a decoration for head and bosom; they now sought diamonds, rubies, emeralds, and pearls. How did they get their wealth? The prime source was the muscles of the fellahin.

As tax gatherers the mamelukes used Coptic scribes. These kept dossiers on each village and were responsible for obtaining the taxes and paying them into the treasury. Often they exploited the peasant's ignorance by making him pay twice over. Often they forced the farmers to sell their cows, their buffaloes, even their straw mats, to produce the piastres required.

The mamelukes also made money out of trade; for though Egypt had lost its central position, the vast increase of trade between Europe and the East insured that some profit came their way. The Egyptian customs had originally been in the hands of Jews, but Ali Bey, an almost independent mameluke chief, ruined them in 1769. Syrian Christians now took their place. Originally a few Syrian families had settled in Cairo in the early eighteenth century; reports of the fortunes to be made swelled their number. Volney states that they had the worst character in the world, being morally far inferior to the Muslims.

The corrupt customs were only one factor in making European merchants find Cairo the most precarious and least agreeable place for advancement in the whole Levant.

Communications were uncomfortable and unsafe. No one had thought to revive the canal which had once linked the Nile to the Red Sea. The only way to travel was by camel caravan. Volney himself journeyed in this way from Cairo to a Suez which he describes as "the place in the world most denuded of everything." His caravan was carrying wood, sails, and ropes for the Suez ships; currency to pay, in Jedda, Mecca, and Mokka, for imports from India and above all for Yemeni coffee. Pilgrims also joined the caravan, since it was safer to journey by sea from Suez than risk the route by Bedouin-infested land.

While Egypt had shrunk in upon itself, the outer world had forged ahead. The English, who were doing much of the forging, had noticed Egypt's position, and toyed with the idea of a shorter route home from the India they now controlled. In 1779 some enterprising British officers organized a convoy to England by way of Suez, Cairo, and Alexandria instead of by sea round the Cape of Good Hope. Two shiploads reached Suez safely; with them they brought some French prisoners of war. The Bedouin of Tor decided to pillage the hopeful travelers. Five leagues from Suez (on a road which takes a twentieth-century motorist around an hour) the party were attacked. Stripped of everything they had, half of them returned to Suez while the others, who had lost their wits with their greatcoats, tried to struggle on to Cairo. The combination of January cold by night and fierce sun by day killed all but one, a French prisoner—"his only shade a thorny bush in which he plunged his head, his only drink his urine." Rescued by an Egyptian fellah who appeared from nowhere on a camel, this M. de Saint-Germain rested three days in the peasant's hut and then continued his journey to Cairo.

One result of this catastrophe was to reduce the importance of the English trading post in Cairo—it specialized in selling small arms and cloth. Volney even hints that the marauding Bedouin had been put up to the attack by officials of the British East India Company in Constantinople. This suggestion is not entirely farfetched. After the recent loss of her North American colonies, Britain's ambitions were largely centered on her new empire in India; the East India Company, a private company with governmental support, had invested vast sums in a trade which went round Africa; the Company was likely to be suspicious of a new short cut to the East which was not under its control. When in the coming century a French entrepreneur, Ferdinand de Lesseps, was to undertake the project of a canal through the Isthmus of Suez, British officials in their embassy in Consantinople were to endeavor to get the Ottoman sultan to suppress it. When the short cut to India had finally been made, Britain was to buy a dominant holding in Suez Canal Company shares and then to station troops alongside its investment. The loss of British interests in eighteenth-century Cairo—where the Venetians continued to sell silk and mirrors and the French to sell goods cheaper than those of their rivals—would have seemed a small price to pay for the continuance of a monopoly in Indian trading.

Volney's concluding impression was that the Egyptians should be pitied, not despised. The fellahin were tough, hard-working people, enduring hardships with great resistance. Rightly directed, their energies could create a much better society. But the major obstacle to progress was a general and total ignorance.

A young French officer, Napoleon Bonaparte, was to be Volney's most attentive and influential reader. Decades later, when his meteoric career was over, when the exiled Emperor of the French could look back on conquests unrivaled since the age of Alexander, "in his first interview with the governor of St. Helena, Napoleon said emphatically: 'Egypt is the most important country in the world.' "[8]

13

Napoleon Through Cairo Eyes

To the people of Cairo June 15, 1798, marked the start of the 1213th year since Muhammad migrated from Mecca to Medina and in so doing initiated the Islamic era.

To the peoples of Europe 1798 marked the fifth year since the execution of Louis XVI of France had confronted the Old World with a militant new republic. In the previous year the twenty-eight-year-old Corsican general Napoleon Bonaparte, armed with proconsular authority from the Directory which now ruled France, had completed the conquest of an Italy which included the Papal States and the half-oriental Venetian republic. It was now expected that France would strike a blow against England, the prime enemy of its republic as it had been the prime rival of its monarchy.

To Napoleon 1798 marked a year of challenge. If he was to do in France what Julius Caesar had done in ancient Rome, he needed some spectacular triumph from which he would return with the means to impose his will. Public opinion believed that Napoleon's equivalent of Caesar's Gaul would be England itself. But Napoleon, who had read Volney's account of Egypt and who in Venice had sniffed the first aromas of the mysterious East, believed that a nation of shopkeepers who were also a nation of brilliant seamen might be perilous to attack at home. He concurred with Talleyrand, the defrocked bishop who directed

French foreign policy, that the shrewdest way to injure England would be by an invasion of Egypt. An almost defenseless province of a ramshackle Ottoman empire, Egypt was halfway to an India where the East India Company had numerous enemies (the chief was Tippoo Sahib of Mysore) only waiting for arms and encouragement to rise against the British. Such rational aims were, as so often in Napoleon's case, confused with visionary dreams. "I saw myself founding a religion, marching into Asia, riding an elephant, a turban on my head and in my hand the new Koran that I would have composed to suit my needs." He would break the power of the mamelukes in Egypt as he had broken the power of the priests in Italy. Alexandria would be made the new capital, not only of Egypt, but of a French empire guiding the three continents of the Old World into a future based on the principles of the Revolution. The Emperor of this new polity would be, of course, Napoleon.

"The time I spent in Egypt," Napoleon was later to say, "was the most beautiful in my life, because it was the most ideal." The year he landed in Egypt was described by a Cairo diarist as "the start . . . of a period of great battles, of ghastly events, of disastrous facts, of frightful calamities, of constantly growing evils, of upsets, of reversal, of continual terror, of revolution, of administrative disorder, of catastrophe, of general devastation: in one word, the start of a whole series of great misfortunes." For once, Arabic hyperbole was almost justified. The writer, Abdul Rahman al-Jabarti, an Azharite graduate of Somali origin, lived through the greatest crisis in Cairo's history since the Ottoman conquest: the arrival in Egypt of the enthusiastic young soldiers of Revolutionary France.

> On Sunday, 10th Muharram, messengers from Alexandria brought news that on Friday, the 8th of the same month, ten English vessels had sailed close enough to the shore to be visible from the town. A little later, fifteen further ships had arrived. The inhabitants of the town were wondering what was afoot when a pinnace put ashore with a party of ten. These presented themselves to the notables of Alexandria, including the governor, Sayid Mohammad Korayim. The strangers declared themselves to be English. They were pursuing, they said, a body of Frenchmen who had sailed, with a considerable fleet, for a destination unknown. They

feared the French purpose might be a sudden attack on Egypt since the Egyptians could neither repel such an attack nor prevent a disembarkation.

Distrusting their words, fearing a trap, the governor gave no ground. The stranger continued: "We shall content ourselves with guarding the city and protecting the coastline; all we ask is food and water, for which we will pay."

"This country belongs to the sultan," the Alexandrines answered. "Neither Frenchmen nor others have concern here. Be so kind as to leave us in peace."

On these words the Englishmen returned to their ships and went elsewhere for their provisions, that "God might achieve the work decreed in his destiny."[1]

This news caused a stir in Cairo. Everyone discussed it, exaggerating greatly.

Three days later it was learnt that the English had sailed away. People calmed down. The self-confident emirs were not worried by these reports. All the Europeans put together could not stand an instant before the mameluke horse, but would be trampled underfoot. On Wednesday, the 20th of the same month, letters from Alexandria, Rosetta and Damanhour announced that two days earlier a very large French fleet had anchored off Alexandria. Some Frenchmen had rowed ashore to contact their consul and other persons. As night fell, some ships moved into Agami where they disembarked men and war matériel. The next morning saw French soldiers as thick as locusts in the city. The Alexandrines, helped by Bedouin, tried in vain to repulse the invaders. They could not. The Bedouin fled while the people locked themselves in their houses. Though they tried to continue the resistance, their lack of preparations and of arms made this a vain attempt. The French then hoisted their flag and summoned the notables. They demanded the surrender of all the arms remaining in the city. Furthermore they insisted that everyone should wear the cockade on his chest. This cockade consists of three pieces of cloth, blue, red and white, worn together in concentric circles.

Al-Jabarti, who was in Cairo throughout these events, describes the consternation in the capital. The two chief emirs, Ibrahim Bey and Murad Bey, reported in haste to Constantinople. Murad

Bey was entrusted with organizing an army to defeat the French. While Murad moved north, his cavalry on the ground, his foot soldiers on the Nile, he ordered the construction of an enormous chain to block the river to French ships.

In the city, directly threatened for the first time since 1517, and by an enemy who was not of the same faith, there was a general panic. The streets were abandoned to thieves and cut-throats. As a countermeasure, to preserve confidence, authorities ordered cafés to stay open and citizens to light lamps in front of their houses and shops.

The first contact with the French came through a written proclamation clandestinely distributed by North African Christians, assembled for this purpose, al-Jabarti believed, in Malta.

It began with the Islamic *bismillah*: "In the name of God, the Merciful, the Compassionate! On behalf of the French nation, founded on liberty and equality, Bonaparte, the great general and commander-in-chief of the French army, proclaims to the entire population of Egypt that for far too long the emirs who rule the country have insulted the French nation and outraged its merchants. The hour of their chastisement has struck. For long centuries this riffraff of slaves purchased in the Caucasus or Georgia have tyrannized the most beautiful country in the world. But God, Master of the Universe and the All-Powerful, has decreed that their reign should cease. People of Egypt! You have been told that I have come here to destroy your religion. It is a lie. Don't believe it. Say to such liars that I am only come among you to seize your rights from the hands of tyrants and restore them to you and that, more than do the mamelukes, I adore God and respect his Prophet and the Koran."

Attached to the rest of this preamble—which continued in the same vein, with the added claim that the French were true Muslims—were certain stipulations: Any village that resisted would be burned; and "the flag of our friend the Ottoman sultan" should be flown beside the tricolor of France.

As in 1517, the Cairenes were spectators of their fate. No one thought to organize them to defend their land. All they could do was pray.

> Since the departure of Murad Bey from Cairo the learned men assembled daily in the mosque of al-Azhar to recite the book of Bokhari[2] for the success of

the Egyptians. The sheikhs of all the religious sects also assembled and offered prayers. So did the pupils in the schools. . . . Groups of ascetics and dervishes processed with flags, making music and praying for victory. Omar effendi, chief of the descendants of the Prophet, issued from the Citadel holding a great flag which the people called the standard of the Prophet and so traversed the city as far as Bulak. He was surrounded by thousands of individuals carrying clubs, making music and shouting prayers.

After this exodus to Bulak, the only people left in Cairo were women, children, and weak old men. They hid themselves in their houses. The streets were empty and dirty, since no one swept or sprayed them any more.

But neither religious faith nor mameluke self-confidence availed against the superior fire power and military training of the French. The mamelukes were routed at Imbaba and "on Tuesday the French entered Cairo and Bonaparte moved into the palace of Mohammad Bey al-Alfi, situated at Ezbekia, in the quarter of al-Sakit. The emir had built this palace, at great expense, the previous year; it was richly furnished." As for the French soldiers, "they chatted good-humouredly with the people and bought at exorbitant prices the things they needed." The cafés and shops reopened. All seemed well.

But as other occupiers of Muslim cities have found on other occasions, resistance soon takes the place of cooperation. The people of Cairo would not long sit quiet under their infidel masters. The inevitable French reprisals destroyed forever the initial harmony between the old Muslims of Muhammad and the new Muslims of European deism. After the first major revolt,

> bands of Frenchmen entered the city at night and penetrated every part. They tore down all barricades they found and assured that everyone was quiet. They then entered al-Azhar mosque with their horses, which they tethered to the prayer-niche; they smashed lamps as well as the night-lights and desks of the students. They looted everything they found in the cupboards; they threw books and the Koran on the ground and trampled them with their boots. They urinated and spat inside the mosque; they drank wine; they smashed bottles which they threw all over the place.

160

They stripped all the people they found there to steal their clothes.

On Friday some of their soldiers stood guard before the entrance to the mosque. The faithful who came to pray fled on seeing them. Other French soldiers patrolled the quarter near the mosque. This quarter, long the most highly regarded in the city, had been avoided by the French during the first days of their occupation. Now it was avoided by Egyptians as the French surged through it by the hundred.

To the unarmed Egyptians the French seemed omnipotent. In fact, since August 1798 they had been in the precarious position of an expeditionary force cut off from their home base. The enormous French invasion fleet (which on open sea covered between two and four square miles) had been told, Napoleon was to argue later, either to put into harbor at Alexandria or return to Adriatic safety in French-occupied Corfu. Instead, Admiral Brueys kept the vast armada anchored in Aboukir Bay, near the site of the ancient Canopic mouth of the Nile. (This mouth had long silted up and as a result Alexandria's importance had decreased while Rosetta, some distance to the east, had become the main port of Egypt.) Nelson's fleet, with better ships, better captains, and better crews had missed the French armada in Malta (where the French knights had surrendered to Napoleon) and had pursued it across the Mediterranean. They caught up with the anchored French ships on the evening of August 1 and at once attacked. By 2 P.M. next day the English fleet was celebrating the total destruction of their enemy's ships. Napoleon's expedition to the Middle East was thus doomed to strategic failure. The Ottoman sultan, instead of welcoming Napoleon's destruction of the mamelukes, declared war on the French republic. Napoleon spent another twelve months in Egypt and Syria, months in which his brutality was displayed in the siege of Acre and in which his idealism was expressed in his schemes for reforming Egyptian society. As a disciple of Volney, Napoleon believed that the native-born men of religion, the *ulema*, could provide a basis for social revitalization. Modern engineering would do the rest. "What could be made of that beautiful country in fifty years of prosperity and good government? One's imagination delights in the enchanting vistas. A thousand irrigation sluices would tame and distribute the overflow of the Nile over every part of the territory. The eight to ten billion cubic yards of water now lost every year to the sea would be channelled to the lower parts of the desert . . . all the way to the oases and even farther west."[3]

But neither savagery in war nor idealism in peace could make the Egyptian campaign more than a sideshow in the war against England and the struggle for power in Paris. In August 1799 Napoleon returned secretly to France. The army he left behind was embittered. Its leaders lacked Napoleon's vision of cooperation with the Muslim majority and began to patronize Syrian Christians and Greeks. During the remainder of the French stay in Egypt—their evacuation was negotiated with the British and the Ottomans in the summer of 1801—the Greek executioner Barthélemy was to be kept busy.

The eighteenth century finished badly. In April 1800 the Muslims got their own back on the Christian collaborators when the French general Kléber, napoleon's successor, went out to defeat an Ottoman force at Mattariya. Kléber regained the city by shelling first Bulak, then Cairo. On June 14 a young Syrian Muslim, Suliman al-Halabi, assassinated Kléber in his garden near Ezbekiah. His motives have been ascribed to fanaticism; more probably they were due to a feeling of Islamic solidarity with a country overrun by infidels. Suliman involved against their will three sheikhs of al-Azhar in his plot. The sentences on the four men adjudged guilty showed a curious departure from the professed aims of the Revolution. The three men of religion were beheaded, while Suliman himself was to have his offending right arm burnt off to the elbow, after which operation he was to be impaled. (The missionaries of the Revolution, which in France had introduced the supposedly humane guillotine, argued that only the traditional punishments would teach the requisite lesson.) Barthélemy (who normally sold glass knick-knacks in a bazaar near Khan al-Khalili) let some of the burning tar fall on the young man's forearm. With extraordinary presence Suliman pointed out that he was exceeding the penalty. During his subsequent impalement, he cried out that he thristed. A French officer, unable to stand the sight, rushed forward with a glass of water. The executioner dashed it to the ground. "Don't do that, sir," he shouted. "The first sip, and he'll be dead." His death took several hours to accomplish.

Kléber's successor, General Menou, tried to placate the Muslims by announcing his own conversion to Islam and removing all local Christians from the government. At the same time he announced that Egypt would become a French protectorate.

The collision of Cairo with the forces of France shows what was to be a continuing pattern. The first effect, it is evident, was opposition to an outside force which could impose its will through superior force.

The second force, however, was no less lasting. This was admiration.

Muslims recognized that at least in its ability to defend itself Islam had fallen behind Europe. Al-Jabarti was an intelligent member of the class which Napoleon had considered the most hopeful in Egypt. He had been educated in the traditional disciplines, unchanged since the days of Nasir Khosrau. The effect of what he saw, as he mixed with the crowds watching the French launch a balloon in Ezbekiah, or as he visited the savants of the Institut d'Egypte, was as decisive as his disgust at the behavior of the soldiers.

In reading his diary it is hard to say which events are the most important; sometimes a trivial incident could be as challenging as something obviously important. The French workers designing the orderly boulevards which Volney had craved used wheelbarrows instead of the primitive carrying bags employed by Egyptians. Windmills were established for grinding corn. "Among other things the French constructed near Ezbekiah a building where ladies and gentlemen met as a certain hour to pass the time and amuse themselves. The spectator paid on going in and needed a ticket to enter." This was "the first service club in history, named *Le Tivoli* after a popular amusement spot in Paris. It offered a dance band (though few partners), billiard tables and other games, a library, the two newspapers published by the army, coffee, European food, a pleasure garden, and similar comforts of home. At the grand opening, the *Courrier de l'Egypte* reports, what 'produced the most agreeable sensation . . . was the presence of fifteen or twenty women dressed with some splendour—an absolutely novel sight in Egypt.' "[4]

But striking though this was in an Egypt where the sexes were so strictly segregated that at weddings it was considered seemly for boys to dance disguised as women, what impressed al-Jabarti most was a French library. In the mansion belonging to the mameluke emir Hasan Kashif,

> the French established a large library with librarians to look after the books and to issue them to those who wanted them. This library opened daily at ten in the morning. The readers assembled in a large room adjoining the room where the books were kept; they sat on chairs round big tables and got down to work. Simple soldiers used to work in this library. If a Muslim wanted to come in, he was in no sense prevented; on the contrary, he was greeted with great friendliness. The French were particularly happy when a Muslim visitor showed himself interested in the sciences; they at once got into discussion with him and showed him all sorts of printed books, with pictures representing different regions of the world, as well as plants and animals.

This library represented the most explosive contribution of the French, not only to Egypt, but the whole Levant. Unlike any conqueror before, Napoleon had taken with him a corps of learned men; these savants produced a lasting memorial in their encyclopedic *Description d'Egypte*. He had also brought with him fonts for printing Greek and Arabic, the two ancient languages of the Middle East. The use of printed books, which even common soldiers could read, was to do more to combat the senescence of centuries than the mameluke defeat.

The French had given the Muslims a tool with which slowly but with increasing momentum they would repair their stagnant society. It would be a tool that would often be used against the French themselves. But a grateful respect for French culture was to be part of most educated Egyptian minds. The fact that French culture came in a lay, not a religious, form made it the more acceptable. The French occupation of Egypt had not lasted long in terms of time. The pattern of love-hate toward the West which it bequeathed would last two centuries at least.

14

Muhammad Ali & Company

E GYPT HAD BEEN THE BACKGROUND of a youthful triumph to Napoleon; as well as memories he took back to Paris new motifs for chair legs derived from the pharaohs. To Egypt Napoleon had been the first boulder in an avalanche of change. Other rocks, stones and pebbles in this avalanche were the members, and enemies, of a dynasty which for better or worse would transform Cairo more radically than any ruler since Saladin.

The founder of this dynasty (whose last representative, the infant son of Farouk I, was deposed in 1953) was Muhammad Ali, the son of a yeoman farmer in what is now northern Greece. He spent a humdrum youth as a tobacco dealer and minor official. In 1798 at the age of twenty-nine he was sent to Egypt as second-in-command of a regiment of volunteers recruited from the Muslims of his district. This district, halfway between Macedonia and Thrace, was the same fringe land between the Aegean Sea and the Balkan mountains which had given birth to Alexander and the Ptolemies. Europeans have usually referred to Muhammad Ali as an Albanian; Egyptians often referred to him as a Turk; he can probably be best described as a Macedonian. The question is unimportant. A man's national status meant less than his religious affiliation in the cosmopolitan Ottoman empire. Muhammad Ali went to Egypt as a Muslim owing allegiance to the Ottoman sultan in Constantinople. Narrowly saved from drowning at the battle of Aboukir by the British admiral's gig, Muhammad Ali did nothing to defeat the French invaders. The next time he stepped on the dry land of Egypt was as Ottoman-appointed pasha in 1801, the year of the French evacuation. The Ottomans were anxious to reassert their control over Egypt now that the French had shot to pieces the mameluke myth. The young man's ambitious nostrils picked up the same scent of possibility as had excited the young slaves from Mingrelia and Georgia. The mameluke beys, divided as ever among themselves, were determined to resist an Ottoman attempt to deprive them of control. Muhammad Ali would introduce into a decade of anarchy two steely constants: his regiment of soldiers and his own ambition. (Loyalty was a constant of no one.) He now sided with the Ottomans (whose writ was his only authority for being in Egypt) and now with the local beys.

At some time between 1801 and 1805 he formulated an ambition which must have been the secret dream of the more ruthless sultans and beys of the past: the total destruction of all rivals and the concentration in his own hands of everything in Egypt. Such an imperious monopoly had been impossible under the Ottoman system. Unwieldy and ramshackle though their empire had become, the Ottomans remained astute into their death-throes. In Egypt they had contrived a sleazy but effective geometry for dividing the rich and exploiting the poor. The pasha with his Ottoman troops formed one angle; the indigenous religious authorities another; the Bedouin could be used at various points as irregular allies; the base was the divisive mameluke caste. The system had been ruinous for Egypt; it has also prevented any one man from concentrating power in his hands.

Muhammad Ali (whose gifts owed everything to instinct, nothing to learning) recognized that the French invasion had shaken the Ottoman reality as much as the mameluke myth; since the Ottomans were farther from Cairo they were the lesser menace; if Egypt were once united, the power of Constantinople could be defeated or kept at bay. But first the mamelukes had to be destroyed. Muhammad Ali proceeded to do this through maneuvers whose brutality and treachery were worthy of the greatest sultans of the past.

The first maneuver took place in 1805; at this time Muhammad Ali's authority as pasha of Egypt was everywhere disputed by the dissident beys. The annual cutting of the dam—due this year on August 17—was used as a decoy. Some of the pasha's agents informed the mamelukes that his presence at the morning ceremony would enable them to seize the unguarded capital. The dam was broken without pomp the previous night while Muhammad Ali secretly posted his soldiers at strategic points. Next morning the mamelukes broke into the city through Bab al-Futuh and paraded with kettledrums. In the narrow street 'Between the Two Palaces' they came under sudden fire. A good number escaped from the trap; those who did not, took refuge in the great mosque of Barkuk. Their fate was dire. Having surrendered, about fifty were stripped naked and murdered on the spot. The remainder were dragged before the pasha. One of the leading beys, goaded beyond endurance by Muhammad Ali's taunts, snatched a dagger from a soldier in a mad attempt to kill the pasha. After this desperate and unavailing act, the remainder were chinned up for the night. In the morning they were treated to an alarming spectacle. The heads of those slain the previous day were skinned in their presence and then stuffed with straw. Except for three beys who were released on payment of ransom, the victims of this sadistic show were tortured and killed that night; their heads, also stuffed with straw, were sent to Constantinople as a sign of Muhammad Ali's power over the beys.

It may seem extraordinary that within six years of this *coup de main* the mamelukes would ride into another trap. Events in the interim, including an attempted British invasion, had blurred remembrance; the collective mameluke mind was inured to violence as a way of life; it lacked imagination to foresee that violence might have a constructive as well as lethal aim.

This time—on March 1, 1811—Muhammad Ali used the excitement of an approaching war in Arabia as his decoy. The Wahhabis were a central Arabian sect who objected to the cult of saints (as popular in Egypt as in Turkey) and who disapproved of such practices as the annual procession of the *mahmal*. They had challenged the authority of the Ottoman sultan in western Arabia by occupying the holy cities of Mecca and Medina as well as the port of Jedda. Muhammad Ali was instructed by the sultan to organize a punitive expedition; it would be led by his favorite son, Tusun. As an inducement to the mamelukes to cooperate, Muhammad Ali had recently restored their fiefs in the Fayum oasis and parts of Upper Egypt.

James Webster, an Englishman who visited Cairo when the events of this March day were fresh in men's minds, has left an account of Muhammad Ali's stratagem.

> His plan was effected on the occasion of a public festival. The Grand Seignor had sent his Kislar Aga to Cairo, as bearer of costly presents to the pasha, and the firman appointing Tusun, the son of Muhammad, to the dignity of a two-tailed pashalik. The same youth had been by his father nominated general of the army of Arabia. The 1st of March 1811 was the day set apart for the investiture of Tusun: and the ceremony was ordered in the Citadel. The principal portion of the Mameluke body, that indeed most conspicuous for its activity and boldness, under Elfi's successor, Shahin bey, had been enticed some time previously into the city, loaded with honors and attentions, and quartered in an appropriated part of the city. These Mamelukes had been invited to take part in the parades and the festivities of the day; and they consented to do so. In the morning Shahin bey with his staff and officers, appareled in whatever they possessed of the greatest cost and magnificence, came to the pasha's hall of audience in the Citadel, to offer their congratulations on so joyous an occasion. Muhammad received them with the greatest affability. They were presented with coffee, and he conversed with them severally, with openness of heart, and serenity of brow. But the serpent lay hidden in its bed of roses!
>
> The procession was ordered to move from the Citadel, along a passage cut in the rock. The pasha's troops moved first, followed by the Mameluke corps. As soon, however, as they had passed the gate, at that end of the rocky passage which leads to the Citadel, it was shut suddenly against the latter, and Muhammad's forces were ordered to the top of the rocks, where they were perfectly secure from the aim of their victims, and whence they leisurely fired upon the defenseless Mamelukes, and butchered them in cold blood, almost to a man; for escape was difficult, that end of the defile

by which they had entered having been also closed, and its breadth, in many parts, being so scanty that two horsemen could with difficulty stand side by side. Of those who were fortunate enough to find shelter in the pasha's harem, in Tusun's abode, and elsewhere, all were dragged forth, conducted before the Kiaya Bey, and beheaded on the spot. The body of the brave leader Shahin was exposed to every infamy. A rope was passed round the neck, and the bloody carcass dragged through various parts of the city, exposed all the while to the execration and the contumely of the inflamed populace. The Citadel itself looked like a hideous slaughter-house, newly deluged with the blood of victims, and overstrown with a multitude of reeking carcasses. Dead steeds lay confusedly along the streets with their golden caparisons soiled in the filthy compound of dirt and gore; their knights, some with limbs hacked off, others without their heads, still clenching their scimitars with the last despairing, yet desperate grasp of death, were flung near their war-horses, prostrate in a black puddle of their own life-blood.

The fiction that one mameluke bey jumped his horse over the walls to safety (he was in fact ill, or suspicious, and stayed at home) inspired many of the painters who furnished the drawing rooms of the dynasty.

Four hundred and seventy mamelukes had been killed in the cowardly slaughter. For two days mameluke property was sacked, including an estimated five hundred houses. Throughout the country orders were given to provincial governors to complete the annihilation of the caste. Some beys escaped to Sudan; others survived in Egypt; but their power was finished.

Muhammad Ali's forceful act made Egypt his own exclusive fief. In theory he remained a vassal of the Ottoman sultan; in reality he was the master of a state in which everyone and everything belonged to him. He did not just own most of the land; he owned it all. His power structure was no different from that of the mameluke sultans of the past. He depended entirely on military force. But instead of relying on bought white slaves (the supply of which was to dry up as Russia took over the Caucasus and as the Balkans became independent) he tried the audacious experiment of training brown-skinned Egyptians to serve as soldiers under European or Turkish officers. The purpose for which he used his soldiers was no different from the purpose of Bibars or Barkuk: he wanted to acquire more territory to provide more money for his estate and his enormous family. (His new harem, a workman confided to a visiting Englishman, was intended to accommodate eight hundred women.) Territory supported military power.

What set Muhammad Ali apart from the mameluke sultans was his enthusiastic acceptance not of Western manners but of Western techniques. (All his life he was particularly impressed by the skills of Frenchmen.) Such an acceptance of the West had been as unthinkable as unnecessary for Bibars and Barkuk. In the late Middle Ages Islamic science remained superior to European; the Ottoman army which had destroyed the mameluke sultanate had been the most formidable military force in Europe, not merely the Middle East. But since the late seventeenth century the Ottoman empire had been humiliated again and again by the technical superiority of European, including Russian, armies. The once irresistible janissaries had become society's reactionary rear guard, not its van. (Inspired by Muhammad Ali's actions against the mamelukes, the Ottoman sultan, Mahmud II, was to deal with his janissaries in similar style.) The great empire of Selim and Suliman had been steadily eroded. At first reluctantly, then with increasing ardor, Ottomans argued for the adoption of Western techniques. As the proud inheritors of a complacent Islam, they felt no need for the Western spirit; they required Western drill and Western arms.

Muhammad Ali's acceptance of the West was limited to those aspects of the society which increased a ruler's power. He had no interest in free political institutions, no concern for human liberties. He wanted a powerful army, and since such an army needed officers he established colleges to produce them: he also sent students to Europe. Foreigners of talent were encouraged to come to Egypt to help construct a modern state. One such was Antoine Clot, a Frenchman of poor family who was born in Grenoble in 1793. Having studied medicine while working as a hairdresser in Marseilles, Clot ran into a French merchant who was a friend of the pasha. The merchant remarked that Muhammad Ali was looking for a doctor to guide the medical services of the Egyptian army. Clot arrived in Egypt in 1825 when Muhammad Ali's considerable, if impermanent, empire was at its height. (At one time or another Egyptian forces, often under the leadership of Muhammad Ali's gifted son, Ibrahim Pasha, controlled Crete, Aden, western Arabia, northern Sudan, Syria, Palestine, and large areas of what is now Turkey.) Clot started a hospital with a medical school at Abuzabel near Cairo. He bravely defied the taboos against dissection (intact since the days of Abdul Latif) and against smallpox introduced vaccination, itself in origin a Turkish practice. His services included combating a cholera epidemic in 1830 and then a bout of plague in 1835. He was created a general in the army, then a bey. Significantly, he was allowed to retain his Christian faith: the regime's encouragement of non-Muslims, including the long-despised Copts, was to be one of its more attractive features. Ironically, the street named in this doctor's honor—a European-style axis providing a link between the railway station and the street leading to the Citadel—became the chief brothel quarter of the city.

Although some of Muhammad Ali's military adventures were against his nominal sovereign, Sultan Mahmud II, both rulers shared similar problems and a similar superficial affection for the West. Both men were to be disappointed. Mahmud II abandoned traditional Turkish costume for braid-edged trousers and fez, introduced Western drill and destroyed the janissaries; Muhammad Ali opened factories, encouraged Western missionaries to bring schools to the Levant, and destroyed the mamelukes. These gestures failed to charm the West. Throughout the century Western influences encouraged the breakup of the Ottoman structure which had started with the revolt of the Greeks; the British used their sea power to strangle Muhammad Ali's burgeoning industrial revolution. This was made possible for them because of Muhammad Ali's position as the nominal subject of the Ottoman sultan. In many ways there is a close parallel between Muhammad Ali's Egypt and the Japan of the Meiji Restoration: the same superficial and rapid westernization, the same local imperialism; Korea, Manchuria, and Formosa were to be the Far Eastern equivalents of Arabia, Sudan, and Syria. Both countries, at their different extremes of the Asian continent, realized the need for industrialization, if the West was to be defied as well as imitated. Yet there was to be one important difference. Japan never recognized outside sovereignty; and Japanese industrialization, however much denounced by the Western countries for its 'unfairness,' was never suppressed. Muhammad Ali's recognition of Ottoman supremacy led directly to the failure of his industrial schemes, under which, if they had succeeded, "Egypt might have emerged into the twentieth century as a small-scale Japan."[1]

In 1838 the Ottoman sultan had granted to the British the right to trade with any of his dominions, freely, without let or hindrance. On paper, this was an excellent extension of the sacred liberal principle of free trade, luckily applying to Egypt, since Egypt was part of the sultan's realms. In fact, this freedom for British traders killed dead the Egyptian industrial system, which at that time was one of the few such systems in existence. For so great was England's start in the industrial race, that all competitors, whether the United States, France, or Germany, were forced to erect protective tariff barriers round their economies, to save their new industries from death in infancy. If Muhammad Ali's industries had been allowed to continue past the intermediate stage, to the stage of graduation, Egypt might have built up an economy partly agricultural, partly industrial. Instead, the Ottoman consent to the principle of free trade allowed British traders to undersell the products of Egyptian industry. Egypt was forced back into the role of a primary producing country. One after another the factories were closed while more and more of the country's land was devoted to the new crop, cotton.

Ottoman attempts at westernization were always one step behind Western ingenuity and greed; its provinces, one after another, became Western colonies, Western protectorates, or pro-Western independent states. By the end of the century Egypt was a virtual protectorate of imperial Britain, while its economy was geared to supplying the mills of Lancashire with cheap raw cotton.

Nevertheless Muhammad Ali and his descendants transformed the structure and appearance of Egypt.

Muhammad Ali modified the structure. He made Egypt an autonomous state, whose rulers could decide for themselves at least on internal change. By building the Mahmudiya canal, named in honor of Mahmud II, he restored the link between the

capital and Alexandria. By so doing he deserves to be ranked as
the second founder of Alexandria, an unimportant fishing village
at the start of his reign. The pasha's effect on Cairo was egotis-
tical. He built a palace at Shubra (the 'island of the elephant'
had now become a solid if rural part of the eastern bank) and
another in the Citadel. He designed a tomb-mosque for himself
which was to dominate the eastern skyline: to Pierre Loti, the
French traveler, it seemed transported bodily from Stamboul.
Otherwise the city remained as unchanged by independence as
Muhammad Ali himself, who retained the Ottoman dress and
manners which he had brought to Egypt.

"In what corner of Grand Cairo I am to seek for grandeur, I
am at a loss to know." The perplexed seeker was an English
traveler, R. R. Madden. A man who enjoyed arraying himself in
Syrian costume, he traveled widely in the Middle East between
1824 and 1827.

> In a city containing three hundred and fifty thousand
> inhabitants, there is not one tolerable street. Splendid
> mosques, some of which surpass, in my estimation,
> those of Constantinople, are built in blind alleys and
> filthy lanes; the public thoroughfares are hardly twelve
> feet wide, darkened by mats to impede the rays of the
> sun, and choked with putrid vegetables and reeking of-
> fals, from the various stalls which line the streets. The
> first thing that astonishes a stranger in Cairo is the
> squalid wretchedness of the Arabs, and the external
> splendour of the Turks. The next thing that surprises
> and confounds him, in every part of Egypt, as well as
> in Cairo, is the manifest opposition of the modes and
> customs of Mahometan countries to those of Christen-
> dom. Here the head is shaved, the beard unshorn; the
> men wear petticoats of cloth; the women trousers of
> silk or cotton. Instead of a hat, a piece of muslin is
> twisted round the head; instead of a surtout, a blanket
> is thrown across the shoulders; a carpet serves for a
> bed; a wooden bowl for a service of plate, a pewter tray
> for a table-cloth; fingers do for forks, and swords for
> carving knives. A man salutes without stooping, sits
> down without a chair, he is silent without reflection
> and serious without sagacity. If you enquire about the
> health of his wife, it is at the hazard of your head; if
> you praise the beauty of his children, he suspects you

of the evil eye. The name of the Prophet is in every man's mouth, and the fear of God in few men's hearts.

Madden visited a lunatic asylum and was horrified by the neglect of the tortured inmates. Their daily nourishment seemed to depend entirely on the gifts of the charitable. If on a particular day no one felt charitable, the lunatics starved. Madden lists the Cairo illnesses in order of their frequency: plague, dysentery, ophthalmia, bilious remittent fever, the ague, and inflammatory fever.

His jaundiced view was shared by James Webster, the visitor of the 1820s whose description of the massacre of the mamelukes has been quoted. From the narrow lanes of Bulak (Webster had made the six-day journey from Alexandria by boat) he crossed an area of open fields to Ezbekiah. (Madden, in Ezbekiah on the day of the cutting of the dam, had seen an area of promenade in the morning, a lake afloat with hundreds of craft in the evening.) Adjoining Ezbekiah was 'the Frank quarter,' where the British consul lived in a secluded lane. Now the Mousky, this area was on the edge of the 'native' town.

> The scenes which the traveller here meets are powerfully opposed to the expectations of the admirer of eastern poetry. Half the inhabitants of the town are so filthy and ragged, that in England they would be sent to the treadmill for indecent exposure. Their dirt is a absolutely indescribable. Few of the streets are wider than 'Change-alley, and they are unpaved and winding. Carriages are never seen. With the thermometer at one hundred and ten, among crowds of Cairenes squeezing and stewing in the avenues, where horses, camels, dromedaries and donkeys, and women muffled and mounted on mules, blocked the place with clouds of small and almost imperceptible dust, which got into our eyes, and the overpowering glare of the sunlight, we had a ceaseless change of temperature at the turn of every street, and the thoughts of the plague, which never leave the imagination of the European. Happy the man who escapes with only bugs and fleas!

Muhammad Ali lost his empire under British pressure in 1841 and his wits in 1848. On his death in 1849 he was succeeded by Abbas, son of his favorite Tusun, who had died aged twenty.

Under Abbas there was a brief reaction against the modernizing policies of Muhammad Ali. Abbas, morosely conservative, reduced the army and closed his father's surviving factories and schools. His death at Benha Palace, not far from Cairo, was to be the most interesting thing about his life.

No one was ever punished for his murder, though two variants of what happened exist. A literary pasha wrote that Abbas perished through his policy of favoring certain of his mamelukes more than others. One current favorite, Khalil Derwish Bey, was unbearably arrogant in his treatment of other young mamelukes in the pasha's employ. These revenged themselves by composing rude nicknames for the favorite. When Khalil reported them to Abbas, they were first flogged, then made to clean up stable ordure in nonmilitary dress. Pardoned, they were brought to Benha to look after the horses. They had neither forgotten nor forgiven their degradation. On the night of July 14, 1854, it was the turn of two youths, Omar Wasfi and Shaker Hussein, to sleep as guards in the pasha's bedroom. The murderers arrived at midnight and were admitted by the young men. When Abbas tried to escape, Omar Wasfi pushed him back into a room full of knives. The death of the pasha was hushed up until his corpse had been taken to his Cairo palace by coach. As against this version, a literary Frenchwoman in a book called *Pulling the Curtain on the Secrets of Egypt* argued that the pasha's maternal aunt, Princess Nazli, arranged the murder. Princess Nazli secured, as bait, two extremely handsome mamelukes and persuaded them to sell themselves in the still flourishing Cairo slave market. As she had foreseen, the pasha's slave buyer was excited by their beauty and bought them for his master's palace. Again as she had foreseen, her royal nephew appointed them to his bedroom rota. At first the mamelukes feared to attack the pasha, a burly man of forty-one; but on their second night of duty they summoned up their courage, did the work they had been paid for, collected their fee, and escaped, one to Albania, another to Constantinople.

Yet even Abbas bequeathed an important innovation to Cairo. Reacting from his grandfather's Francophilia—Madden had described Muhammad Ali as being "surrounded by a vile set of Frank advisers, the very scum of Genoa and Marseilles"—Abbas favored the Anglo-Saxons. He encouraged Samuel Shepheard to found a hotel which was to become almost as famous as the pyramids. He gave the British permission to start work on a railway to link Alexandria and Cairo. As a result his corpulent uncle Said, who reigned from 1854 to 1863, could visit his estates in a one-car railway train decorated with arabesques and furnished with dark leather sofas. Said's name was to be connected with another mode of transport. Against British opposition, he gave Ferdinand de Lesseps a concession to drive a canal through the Isthmus of Suez; the northern terminal, Port Said, was to be named in his honor. Thus Abbas and Said, through railway and canal, put Egypt back where it had been before the voyage of Vasco da Gama: at the center of world communications.

The man who was to exploit this new strategic importance as well as the new crop, cotton, grown since Muhammad Ali's day, but increasingly important, was the son of Ibrahim Pasha, Ismail. He would transform the appearance of Egypt and make Cairo what it fundamentally is today. In a reign which lasted from 1863 to 1879 Ismail spent lavishly on all the appurtenances of a modern state from lighthouses to post offices, from schools for girls to hotels for Europeans.

In 1866 S. S. Hill, author of *Travels in Egypt and Syria*, traveled from Alexandria to Cairo. He put up at a Coptic house in the same fringe area where Webster had found the British consul. Visitors were still not a common sight. A crowd of some two hundred people loitered outside, curious to behold a foreigner. But things had begun to change. Hill drove out to Shubra "to inspect the pasha's palaces and gardens." After leaving the city gate he was much inconvenienced by clouds of dust blowing from the northeast; also by the sun. These inconveniences were of brief duration, "for at hardly one-eighth of a mile from the gate we entered an avenue of acacia and sycamore trees, such as would ornament the vicinity of any capital city in the world. This avenue extends the whole distance from where we entered it to the palace and gardens we were about to visit. The road is a raised way for about half the distance over a fertile plain. . . . On our way we met several hundred donkeys loaded with panniers of chopped straw, which is the usual substitute for hay in Egypt, and a long string of camels loaded with many articles of consumption for the town."

The lake by whose borders the beys had built their houses, where Napoleon had lodged and where in the dry season his soldiers had drilled, had been finally drained and turned into a park.

> The great square of Ezbekiah, which we now entered, is remarkable for its open and cheerful character, and wants only the moving scene of a similar place in any city in Europe to display many of the appendages to refinement during the hours of relaxation. But what it presented now it presents at all hours. The pasha and his predecessors have here planted shrubs and laid out walks, and made avenues of the fresh circassia, and thus given form to the ready materials, before the elements that should animate the square are yet conceived. It forms a nearly square space of about a mile and a half, where on all sides are seen to the best advantage some of the finest edifices in Cairo, including a military college, and a long line of ancient houses, evidently the residences of families in easy circumstances. Between the houses and the walks there is a broad road, where may be often seen a stately Arab on horseback, attended by one or two servants on foot, and a *says*, or hostler, who precedes him. Dikes have been raised to form a canal that receives the waters of the Nile, which circulate round the place when the inundations have attained a considerable height; but this again becomes dry when the Nile is lower. The walls on the bank of the canal have been planted with trees, which now flourish in all their freshness and beauty.

The culmination of Ismail's extravagant reign was the inauguration of the Suez Canal in 1869. To mark the linking of two seas Ismail planned an Opera House which would provide Ezbekiah with the animation so desired by Mr. Hill. To mark the return of Egypt to the center of the world, Giuseppe Verdi was asked to compose an opera with an imperial Egyptian theme; in the event, *Aida* was late, and *Rigoletto* was performed instead. More important to Ismail (under whose reign Europeans had flooded into his country) was the presence of the most glamorous European of all, the Empress Eugénie of France. He housed this lady in a palace which an aesthete would describe as "of doubt-

ful taste but madly sumptuous"[2] but which probably impressed
the wife of Napoleon III. The palace was built on the 'middle island,' known generally as Gezira (or island) and, in its northern
sector, Zamalek, after some little shacks which Muhammad Ali
had first had built there. For the use of Ismail—now reigning
with Ottoman permission as a hereditary viceroy, or khedive—
there were main Cairo palaces at Abdin and Ismailiya: "and beyond the limits of the metropolis the names of these gorgeous
mansions is legion. At Kasr al-Nil and all along the neighboring
banks of the Nile, on the islands of Roda and Gezira, at Giza,
Abbasiya, Shubra—everywhere rise the unsightly and ill-built
palaces in which viceregal extravagance and ostentation have
found an outlet. Not one of all these huge buildings is other than
an eyesore. Not one is tastefully furnished. The khedive's reception room at Abdin Palace used to be a monument of the mere-
tricious style which rejoices in gold and crimson and pier-
glasses."[3] Ismail's civil list ran to £700,000 or about
$3,500,000 a year—twice as much as Queen Victoria's.

Ismail had been able to afford these extravagant whims—and
the receptions to mark the opening of the Canal were triumphs
of gastronomical overindulgence—thanks to a world shortage of
cotton resulting from the American Civil War. Not only was
Egypt again at the center of the world; she was also the provider
of the 'long staple' of civilized dress. The value of her cotton crop
soared from five million to twenty-five million pounds sterling. In
order to diffuse European ideas, in order to make true his boast
that Egypt now belonged to Europe, not Africa, Ismail had apparent allies in the scores of thousands of Greeks, Italians,
Marseillais, to say nothing of Lebanese, who flooded to the El-
dorado by the Nile. These foreign communities inhabited new
quarters that sprawled on the once silt-land between Ezbekiah
and the Nile. There were Italianate palazzi for the rich with
gardens where solemn green mango and vivid oranges collected
the omnipresent dust; for the poorer migrants there were houses
built after the worst pattern of a fifth-rate artisan's suburb.[4]

This influx of Europeans—no fewer than eighty thousand arrived in Egypt in 1865[5]—had a revolutionary effect on the Egyptian capital. For six centuries Cairo had been divided between
the mamelukes and the Egyptians; they had lived, in greater or
less comfort, in one city; palace rubbed shoulders with hovel; in

the mosque the bey and the beggar were temporarily one. Now for the first time a new phenomenon appears: two Cairos coexisting on one site, an Egyptian Cairo and a European Cairo, joined by nothing but the tolerance of the khedive.

The Egyptian Cairo continued to live as before: not only neglected, it was increasingly destroyed. The modernizing authorities drove new thoroughfares through ancient beauties (like the dreary Muhammad Ali Boulevard linking the Citadel to Ezbekiah); if such European straight lines destroyed irreplaceable mosques and palaces the authorities were not disturbed. Ismail's Minister of Public Instruction, Ali Mubarak, asked rhetorically: "Do we need so many monuments? Isn't it enough to preserve a sample?" Since Bab Zuweyla had been a place of execution, he suggested that, like the Bastille, it should be destroyed.

The Egyptian Cairo became a place for tourists and sensation-hunters.

The slave market still existed in the 1860s. It was worse stocked than before.

> The most beautiful women were formerly brought from Georgia and Circassia; but this trade ceased with the independence of Greece, and the pashas and beys, with the exception of some of the more wealthy who still obtain Circassians by way of Constantinople, have been since that time obliged to content themselves with the rather tawny Abyssinians, which are brought down the Nile in plenty, and may, when not especially handsome, and before they have been, as the custom is, trained to some occupation, such as sewing, and the housewife's accomplishments, generally be purchased for the moderate sum of about four purses, which is equal to twenty pounds sterling.

Boys were still castrated, their compensation a life of ease and prestige.

The government of Ismail, anxious to impress the West that a modern kingdom now ruled the Nile from Alexandria to Khartoum, hardly bothered with the quarters where most people lived. Hill gives us memorable word pictures to set beside the more tender lithographs of David Roberts. One is from the Mokattam heights.

All is uniform in colour, and of the same shade as the desert, from the roofless dwellings of the artisans to the comparatively grand dwellings of the proudest and most opulent citizens; and even the mosques and the minarets that adorn the town, exhibiting the same feature of common decay, are tinged with deathlike tints of the desert. Some of the minarets do not even stand erect, while others are shattered as if they had been struck by cannon balls.

Hill then descends into the streets which he had seen from above. An utter dereliction is their common trait:

Walking through the streets of Cairo, one cannot fail to be struck by the utter want of uniformity or even of completeness in its buildings. If the front is complete, one of the sides or the back has fallen in, or the upper story has not been finished. Hundreds of houses are even seen wanting their whole fronts, while of many, some of the beams have fallen at one end and some at the other, and now rest on the floor of the apartments to which they once formed the roof.

In these areas of Cairo—the word *baladi* (village) came to be used to differentiate them from the *frangi* areas of European influence—the ancient customs of the city continued. Women hid their faces. Gérard de Nerval described nineteenth-century Cairo as the city of the East where women were most hermetically veiled; in a month spent in Cairo Webster had not seen "the face of a single woman of any age in the street, nor any one from the window, save those by whom I was spitten upon." The life of the family was interior, lived in courtyards which could be described poetically:

The inner court is almost as silent and deserted as the guarded windows which overlook the street. We shall see nothing of the domestic life of the inhabitants; for the women's apartments are carefully shut off from the court, into which open only the guest rooms and other masculine and semi-public apartments. After the bustle of the street this quiet and ample space is very refreshing, and one feels that the Egyptian architects have happily realised the requirements of eastern life. They make the streets narrow and overshadow them with projecting meshrebiyas, because the sun beats down too fiercely for the wide streets of European towns to be endurable. But they make the houses themselves spacious and surround them with courts and gardens, because without air the heat of the rooms in summer would be intolerable. The eastern architect's art lies in so constructing your house that you cannot look into your neighbour's windows, nor he into yours; and the obvious way of attaining this end is to build the rooms round a high open court, and to closely veil the windows with lattice blinds, which admit a subdued light and sufficient air, and permit an outlook without allowing the passing stranger to see through. The wooden screens and secluded court are necessary to fulfil the requirement of the Mohammadan system of separating the sexes.[6]

Life was not always as maidenly as this.

Religion, which restricted social life, also gave occasions when it could be indulged. Cairo was famous for its *moulids*, or fiestas connected with the memories of holy men or women. The purpose of a *moulid* was "to glorify God by venerating one of His favorites." The custom of such veneration went back to Fatimid times. Cairo was fortunate in possessing the relics of more of God's favorites than any other Muslim city. The head of Ali's son, Hussein, was buried in a mosque within a stone's throw of al-Azhar; his sister, Sayida Zaynab, was buried in a mosque restored by Abbas Pasha near where the canal had originally branched from the Nile. Three of Hussein's children were buried in the city. Other descendants of the Prophet were joined by a host of holy or outstanding men. Each of these *moulids*—as late as 1938 seventy-eight such fiestas were known to a Scottish connoisseur[7]—was given over to festivities which included transvestite dancing and great deal of noise.

Throughout the nineteenth century the ancient customs connected with the pilgrimage and the cutting of the dam continued unspoiled. Let us hear for the last time (the custom would not outlast that century) an account of the breaching of the Nile:

During the day which precedes the cutting away of the obstructions to the passage of the water, boats gather about the entrance of the Canal, upon the Nile. Towards evening the river between Bulak, the port or quay of Cairo, and the mouth of the Canal, which is

182

about a mile, the water exhibits a scene of gaiety, from
the greater part of the boats being very pleasant craft.
. . . After the departure of the daylight on this evening,
some fireworks are exhibited; but the more grand ban-
quets are reserved for the moment of opening the
Canal, which, however, is at an hour that renders their
effect quite negative. The pasha, who presided on the
important day of this opening, arrived with his suite at
about half past nine o'clock in the morning, and, after
passing through a double file of soldiers, dismounted,
and took the chief seat in a large tent, reserved for
those who were willing to pay for their places of distinction. His Highness took his place with some ceremony, but by what means he communicated his com-
mands to cut the dike I did not perceive. The work
was, however, speedily commenced, and coins were
thrown into the deep, but yet dry, Canal, and scram-
bled for by one or two hundred persons, who had descended the banks, until the water rushing down, as if
forced, at first its slow, but afterwards its quicker,
passage, carried some of the party off their legs, and
obliged them to swim to recover the shores, which are
accessible on either side. The crowd of spectators on
this occasion was very great. Some persons estimated
their number at from 10,000 to 15,000; but I saw only
one or two of the fair sex among them, and these, to
judge from their dress, were quite of the lowest order.[8]

With the speed of the Nile bursting the eroded dam, the Egypt
of Ismail was to gallop toward disaster. The two communities
which had been living in apparently friendly coexistence—the
Europeans and the Egyptians—were to become masters and
servants, rulers and ruled.

The khedive's extravagance could not survive the slump in cotton prices when, after the victory of the North, America began
exporting southern cotton once more. Ismail's foreign creditors
would not put up with promissory notes. The force of an all-
powerful Europe moved in to secure the settlement of Ismail's
mountainous debts.

Ismail, desperate for money, now resorted to methods of taxation which reduced the standard of living in his kingdom to that
of a concentration camp. Ismail the Magnificent, now known as
Ismail the Spendthrift, was bundled off the throne by the real

owners of Egypt, the European moneylenders. The son installed to replace him, Towfik, became the enemy of the Egyptians whose material interests had suffered from Ismail's extortions and whose pride now suffered from Towfik's subservience to European advisers.

An army revolt led by Orabi Pasha, a proto-Nasser of the nineteenth century, came near to succeeding. Its basic aims were to introduce some form of parliamentary government to give expression to the wishes of the Egyptian people. It opposed the whole Turco-Circassian pyramid, of which the royal family was the apex.

Just as the British had thwarted Muhammad Ali's attempts to industrialize Egypt, so now for similar reasons they defeated Orabi's attempts to democratize the country. Under the Liberal government of Gladstone, British forces landed in Alexandria and proceeded to restore the khedive to his full prerogatives. The occupation, the Liberal government insisted, would be strictly "temporary." Next year, the year after, soon, sometime, the soldiers would be withdrawn. Meanwhile, the Egyptian ministry had a British adviser whose word was law. The military occupation was in fact to last more than seventy years and to end only with the dynasty it supported.

Now that Egypt was virtually a British protectorate—sharing the colonial status forced by the 'Franks' on all the major Muslim countries with the exception of the rump of the Ottoman empire—the European quarter of Cairo became supreme. The Cairo which has been the subject of this book resembled the old quarter of a city in French North Africa, the native town kept as a picturesque adjunct to the new.

"What is this? Where are we fallen?" asks Pierre Loti in 1907. "Save that it is more vulgar, it might be Nice, or the Riviera, or Interlaken." Loti visits the Muhammad Ali mosque. "Soldiers are on guard there—and how unexpected are such soldiers in this holy place of Egypt. The red uniforms and the white faces of the north: Englishmen billeted in the palace of Muhammad Ali."

The pyramids and the Sphinx have become properties for the tourists of Thomas Cook; the descendants of the Fatimids, tourist guides. Pierre Loti describes one area near the pyramids at the height of Europe's 'belle époque':

The tourists who have come tonight, and upon whom have pounced the black-cloaked Bedouin guides, wear cap and ulster or furred greatcoat: their intrusion here seems almost an offence; but, alas, such visitors become more numerous in each succeeding year. The great town hard by—which sweats gold now that men have started to buy from it its dignity and its soul—is become a place of rendezvous and holiday for the idlers and upstarts of the whole world. . . . Little more than a mile away there ends a road travelled by hackney carriages and tramway cars, and noisy with the delectable hootings of smart motor cars; and behind the pyramid of Cheops squats a vast hotel to which swarm men and women of fashion, the latter absurdly feathered like redskins at a scalp dance; and sick people of a purer air; and consumptive English maidens; and ancient English dames, a little the worse for wear, who bring their rheumatisms for the treatment of the dry winds.

If Europeans could so upset a Breton naval officer, their effect on the native Egyptians was yet more traumatic.

Ahmed Amin, an Egyptian writer, tells how he lived as a child near a British camp; his house adjoined the ground where they played football and cricket. "I was so terrified of their red coats, blue trousers and general bearing that I usually changed my route whenever I saw them coming. My father's view of them was no more rational, but typical of the people's philosophy of surrender. The soldiers were the symbols of God's anger. The Egyptians had oppressed each other for a long time and had forgotten God's laws. The English were God's hand of revenge. They were here to torture and torment them until they saw God's path."

A new generation was to see in Egyptian nationalism the path of God; resistance would take the place of surrender.

15

Fifty-Fifth Century

CAIRO'S WEST-BANK PRECURSOR, MEMPHIS, had symbolized a human as well as an Egyptian revolution. Uniting Upper and Lower Egypt, it was also the first metropolis created after men had changed from gathering food (whether by picking fruit or knocking down game) to growing cereals in orderly fields and then storing them in barns. Since the barns were vulnerable to attack, they required a more organized defense force than had existed before. A food-growing society thus forms the background to this book or is implicit in its story. Cairo's triumphs, and its imports, depended on the delta's agricultural wealth; its defeats were prompted by the desire of outsiders to possess this cornucopia, and its people's miseries resulted from a Nile too abundant, or too mean.

Its fifty-fifth century was destined to transform the city at the apex of the delta, ending many of its previous constants. For this century—the twentieth after the Christian revelation, the fourteenth after the coming of Islam—brought a revolution as fundamental as that which had turned casual hunters into serious farmers.[1]

The industrial and technological revolution first achieved in the West and then exported to the East was to transform most aspects of Egyptian life.

185

Lord Cromer, the British proconsul who ruled Egypt during the first quarter century of direct European control, claimed in 1901 that "the foundations on which the wellbeing and material progress of a civilised community should rest have been laid." In this two-volume apologia, he congratulated "a small body of Englishmen who, in various capacities, and with but little direct support or assistance from their Government or its representatives, have of late years devoted their energies to the work of Egyptian regeneration," on having abolished the whip as an instrument of government, and on having all but abolished slavery and forced labor.

But European engineers achieved more fundamental changes than the measures of politicians, which were superficial in many cases and unpopular in others.

Until the nineteenth century, Egyptian irrigation had consisted in the diversion of the summer flood through canals which flooded the fields for some months and then left them so steeped in moisture as to grow one crop. Nothing could be done to store the water for another season. Muhammad Ali had seen the need for a series of weirs at the start of the delta. These would hold back the water and release it when required; otherwise much flowed wasted into the sea. A scheme for a delta barrage had been designed by a French engineer, Mougel bey, but because of lack of money, official support and technical expertise, this visionary scheme (it proposed to retain the waters of the Rosetta and Damietta branches and release them through three canals) was not put into full effect until 1890. In that year a team of British engineers completed Mougel bey's barrage in an architectural style recalling the Waverley novels of Sir Walter Scott. Although the Barrage gardens became one of the most attractive places for picnics near Cairo, the British had not planned to amuse the Cairenes. They had aimed to increase the yield of cotton in the Delta fields, and in this aim (connected with the needs of the Lancashire cotton mills) they succeeded.

For Cairo the taming of the Nile to the south of the city was more important. In 1902 two other great weirs were established across the Nile: one at Assiut and the other at Aswan. The Aswan dam, the work of Sir William Willcocks, was one of the engineering marvels of its day. The effect of the two dams was to diminish the age-old dependence on summer floodwater. As a result the ancient Cairo canal was earthed in and transformed to an ugly boulevard, the Street of the Cairo Canal. In 1957 it was renamed Port Said street (Sharia Bor Said) after the target of the last British attempt, in November 1956, to regain control of Egyptian destinies.

The taming of the Nile (a process to be developed throughout the century, and to culminate in the building of the High Dam in the 1960s) abolished the need for sebeels, the caste of water sellers, and the annual ceremonies connected with the flood. The cisterns no longer echoed to female gossip; the water sellers took to selling soft drinks; and the Nilometer became a museum.

The other great ceremony of the Cairene year, the start of the pilgrimage to Mecca, fell victim to a mixture of politics and progress. The defeat of the Ottoman empire in the First World War balkanized the Middle East. In the region of the Holy Places there was no geographical expression of Islamic unity. Separate sovereign states (including the new settler-state of Israel) controlled the land route to western Arabia. The holy cities of Mecca and Medina, part of Saudi Arabia since 1926, were ruled by Wahhabis who disapproved on principle of such customs as the *mahmal*. In the realm of progress, new methods of transport made possible the 'instant pilgrimage,' lacking the dangers and the contemplative broodings of the past.

But the most dramatic change was wrought, unwittingly, by the Egyptian successors of Antoine Clot. Clot bey had worked for the Egyptian army, but his disciples worked for the Egyptian people. They accomplished changes more revolutionary than the taming of the Nile. They tamed the diseases that had previously reduced the population of Egypt to a fraction of what it had been under the Ptolemies. During the nineteenth century the population of Cairo had grown from around 250,000 at the time of Napoleon to nearly 400,000 at the turn of the century. Its pace suddenly quickened. By the late 1960s it had multiplied tenfold. The suburb of Shubra—the island that had grown round the shipwrecked *Elephant*, the country village to which nineteenth-century citizens rode out to escape from city cares—alone housed one million people. This was only the beginning of a violent increase in population, which proved more destructive of ancient Cairo than the town planning of the previous century. Medical progress was only one cause of the sudden growth. The fellahin increasingly preferred the amenities of life in a city slum to existence in an impoverished village. Like logs taken over by wasps, Cairo's constituent cities, European as much as Egyptian, were colonized by country folk who poured into the capital and by their babies who did not die. Palazzi, which in the 1880s had housed the families of European immigrants, cotton brokers and advisers, merchants and entrepreneurs, became divided and subdivided. The cool, stone-built mansions so lovingly described by romantic travelers lost their eastern calm as two dozen families shared their space. Under this pressure the separation between *frangi* and *baladi* disappeared. The flat roofs of thirtyish blocks sustained new *baladi* quarters, villages of huts complete with hens and sheep living a rural life high above the traffic. In the outlying suburbs, where Italianate villas once lined leafy streets, a surge of shoddy building created one of the world's largest urban deserts. The *art nouveau* palace of Habib Sakakini (rumored by its credulous neighbors to be set on a revolving metal plate that could catch the right breeze) was beset by tenements. Many new buildings were cemented with too much sand and their collapse, killing owners and tenants, became a regular feature in the daily press. For with the Nile tamed, it was possible to build wherever the land was flat. A new northern suburb, Heliopolis, linked to the city by a tram and known in Arabic as 'New Cairo,' had been conceived in the first decade of the twentieth century by a Belgian baron who built his own palace in imitation of a Hindu temple, though he furnished its interior in solid Brussels comfort. Maadi, southern equivalent of Heliopolis, had been connected to Cairo by a railway. But these two suburbs, intended for the well-to-do, were inundated by the same *baladi* flood that overwhelmed Mattariya in the north and Giza in the west. The trees shading the highway along which Empress Eugénie had ridden to visit the pyramids were uprooted; the fields that had glistened emerald through their boles were made coarse with brick; slums, old their first year, mushroomed behind a façade of inelegant nightclubs. For the first time the heights of Mokattam were built upon, by the wealthy in flight from the poor; the City of the Dead shared its haunted thoroughfares with the raucous living.

The proliferation of people affected the spirit as well as the appearance of Cairo. Numbers, as much as Western influence, destroyed the harem and its twin symbols of the grille over windows and the veil over faces. The segregation and veiling of women, no more part of pre-Islamic Arabia than of Pharaonic Egypt, had never been practicable in crowded villages, where women had toiled in the fields alongside men. It had flourished in towns where there was space for women to be secluded. Crowded Cairo made the veil impossible. Female emancipation advanced as the population increased. In 1900 the veil had been universal; by the 1960s it was a rarity. However, in the 1970s, a sense that Westernization had perhaps taken Egyptians too abruptly from their roots induced a proportion of women to adopt a new headgear. This covered the hair and shoulders with a rounded bonnet and neck scarf but left the face unveiled.

The spectacular expansion of Cairo (reflected to a lesser degree by all Egyptian cities) had other repercussions.

The old upper class, based on country fiefs, yielded physical and political ground to movements voicing the surging opinion of the towns. During the final years of Occupation the Arabic press had expressed a national resistance to foreign or upper-class control; the spread of education gave its journalists a growing audience. The nationalist movement of the 1920s, led by Saad Zaghlul, could count on a far more coherent and organized support than the venture of Orabi, scotched by the British and the Palace in collusion. Zaghlul's program of constitutional nationalism enjoyed a support too wide to be suppressed, even though the British prevented him from being prime minister for more than a matter of months. After his death, his party, the Wafd, suffered from a third-generation deterioration. During the Second World War his successor, Mustafa Nahas, lost popular support when he agreed, on foreign insistence, to head the government. (This insistence was brutally expressed. The British plenipotentiary invaded Abdin Palace with tanks and demanded that King Farouk, then popular, abdicate or accept Nahas as prime minister.) Yet some of Zaghlul's ideals were to triumph in the 1952 revolution led by Gamal Abdul Nasser and proclaimed over the radio by Anwar Sadat. In form this revolution was a *coup d'état,* not a popular rising. The military elements that ensured its success were to hamper its progress. In particular they were to deny it the constitutional aspects implicit in Zaghlul's policy. A fear of foreign intervention, an uncertainty of his own people, and a suspicious temperament, allowed Nasser to sponsor a system in which the secret police became all-powerful, and in which the army became a state within the state. Yet Nasser was far more than a Latin American caudillo. His resistance to the Palace, the old upper class and their foreign supporters, expressed the consensus of Egyptians. Many of his measures were beneficial to the country, and his defiant foreign policy enhanced Arab pride and made Egypt a leader of the Third World. The extent of his popular backing was shown, not when he successfully nationalized the Suez Canal in 1956, but at the most disastrous moment of his career.

Nasser's sternest criticism of King Farouk had been the comparative failure of his war on behalf of the Palestinian Arabs in 1948. Yet in June 1967 Nasser's expensive new air force was annihilated on the ground by an Israeli preemptive strike. In a catastrophe rivaling Orabi's defeat at Tel al-Kebir, the Egyptian army abandoned Sinai, leaving the Israelis to seize large tracts of territory previously ruled by Egypt's allies, Syria and Jordan. A new wave of Palestinians were forced out of their country. On June 9, for good or bad, the people of Cairo played a decisive role in their own history; something they had rarely done before. The city that had sighed for Tumanbey but cheered Selim, that had prayed against the French but taken no part in the Battle of Imbaba, heard and saw—for television had reached the Nile—their president offer his resignation. A society that worshipped success would have spurned Abdul Nasser. But this city had endured foreign rule for centuries and could endure it no more. As the citizens of Tel Aviv danced to the news of Nasser's fall, people in Cairo crowded the new streets and the old, the *baladi* quarters and the *frangi*, demanding that, precisely because the foreigners wanted Nasser to go, Nasser should stay. He was the first native-born Egyptian in history to rule the east-bank city, the first Egyptian to rule Egypt since the later pharaohs. The conquest of the myth that Egypt must be ruled by foreigners meant as much as the conquest of the Nile. We have another picture to balance this one. In November 1977 the same city welcomed Nasser's successor, Sadat, on his return from Jerusalem. After the crossing of the Canal in 1973, many Egyptians were prepared to accept a just peace.

This book will have made evident the complexity of Egypt and of its capital; complex motives prompted this acceptance of a move that temporarily isolated the largest Arab state from most of its partners.

The increased population could no longer live off agriculture alone. More important than flamboyant actions or defiant words were economic realities. By the 1960s the area of arable land was hardly greater than in the days of Cromer; the mouths dependent on what it produced had multiplied fourfold. The regime that Nasser overthrew had squandered its capital abroad or invested it in enterprises bringing quick profit but employing few workers. Unfortunately, industrialization came a century too late. Its growing pains could more appropriately have been surmounted in the nineteenth century, had Europe allowed Muhammad Ali's factories to function. Although Nasser's new republic could ensure that the diversion of surplus labor to manufacture was no longer thwarted, it could less easily overcome inefficiency, shoddiness, and waste, particularly as it chose to rely on military officers to run factories staffed by rural recruits lacking the perfectionism of their rivals in Hong Kong or Singapore. Factories producing cement, automobile tires, steel, and refrigerators turned Helwan, an Edwardian spa twenty miles south of Cairo, into a proletarian city whose chimneys polluted a dry salubrious air once rivaling Aswan's. A reluctance to go far from Cairo decided planners against locating the new industries in the remoter desert. But the products of Helwan and other industrial suburbs were often inferior to those manufactured abroad. One result of Nasser's austere if inspiriting years was a widespread craving for imported goods.

When he succeeded Nasser in 1970, Sadat was determined to avoid his predecessor's most criticized mistakes; he needed to form a base for his own popularity. Dismantling much of the police-state apparatus, he rejected at the same time the controlled economy whose weakness had left it few and irresolute defenders. Internally he fostered a religious rather than an Arab Nationalist ideology, and in foreign affairs turned to the West at the expense of the Soviet Union. More important for Cairo, he initiated on 'Open-Door' policy, facilitating the importation of consumer goods and at the same time enriching the importers. New boutiques bulged with expensive trash; foreign cars congested the narrow streets; a new class richer than Muhammad Ali's beys and more odious than Nasser's mamelukes did little to conceal a wealth that owed nothing to productivity or education. At one time, native Egyptians had consisted of al-Azhar scholars, small traders, and fellahin. Now they formed classes set apart by an abyss of money. The existence of a plutocracy lacking Eastern or Western manners posed the question of whether, or how, the new Cairo could overcome such extreme divisions. It could, like Beirut or Teheran, simply explode; or its immemorial tradition of restraint could control and tax the arrogantly rich.

Besides being a market for imports, in a grave innovation the Cairo of the late 1970s became a labor exchange for human exports. Egyptians had traditionally stayed at home. The country had perhaps the lowest quota of emigrants for any nation of its size. Only pashas, diplomats, and students had gone abroad previously. Now the new wealth in adjacent countries emptied Cairo of its artisans. This had happened on a small scale once before, when Sultan Selim took Egyptian workmen to embellish his capital. They had gone cursing and had left Constantinople at the first opportunity. But now Egyptian youth besieged embassies for visas by the hundred thousand. They would bring back, apart from such inessentials as Afro hairdos and alien tastes in music, new ideas for running a country.

In the long run the effect of these migrating millions was likely to modify whatever shape and form the new Cairo assumed. In the interim a lack of people who could plane a shelf, mend a fuse, or install a bath-plug made the Cairo of the 1970s an inconvenient place in which to live. Vehicles replaced, as scatterers of pedestrians, the past's turbaned horsemen, and trashy boutiques the sellers of water, from which all things live.

Notes

1   MOTHER OF THE WORLD

1 The initial letter *q*, usually dropped in spoken Egyptian Arabic, is always pronounced in al-Qahira. Al-'Ahira would mean 'the prostitute.'
2 Stanley Lane-Poole, *The Story of Cairo*.
3 In Nubia, at Kalabsha, the cliffs are only 170 yards apart.
4 Abdul Latif al-Baghdadi, *The Eastern Key* (trans.).
5 Jacob Burckhardt, *The Age of Constantine*, p. 101.

2   MEMPHIS AND HELIOPOLIS

1 C. J. R. Haswell, *Bull, Soc. Géog. d'Egypte*, II, 1922.
2 Abdul Latif al-Baghdadi, *op. cit.*
3 Emir Sayf al-din Omari.
4 The modern university of Ain Shems preserves, in Arabic, this name.
5 Max Muller, *The Mythologies of All Races*, vol. 12, p. 31.
6 The earlier buildings of Sumer and Ur in Iraq were made of brick.
7 Jean Philippe Lauer, *Sakkarah, les Monuments de Zoser,* quoted in K. Lange and M. Hirmer, *Egypt: Architecture, Sculpture, Painting in 3000 years.*

3   BABYLON-IN-EGYPT

1 The friendliness between Greek and Hebrew did not last into the Roman period. Vespasian, whose son Titus was to fulfill

Christ's prophecy of the destruction of Herod's temple, closed the temple at Leontopolis. A Jewish massacre of Greeks in the reign of Hadrian led to the reduction of the Jewish community in Alexandria. The Greek acceptance of Christ as the Messiah finally alienated Greek from Jew.

2 Matthew 2:15 recalls Hosea 11:1.

3 I Peter 5:13.

4 This convenient term is a medieval European derivative of the Arabic word *Qibt*, which itself derives from the middle syllable of the Greek word Αιγυπτιοι, meaning Egyptians.

4 FUSTAT

1 K. A. C. Creswell, Early Muslim Architecture.

5 IBN TULUN

1 Sited on bedrock above the Nile flood, Fustat had an intricate drainage system of channels and pits. Later precincts had lamentably poor drainage, which, like that of Paris and London, was not improved until the latter half of the nineteenth century.

2 About AD 1296.

3 Creswell, *op. cit.*, p. 305

4 With the exception of four Byzantine columns which frame the chief prayer niche, which is itself lined with colored marbles of a later date.

6 FATIMID CAIRO

1 The site of the present al-Aqmar mosque.

2 Near the site of the present railway station square.

3 The story is quite possibly apocryphal. Evidence that it may be an archetypal myth appealing to some Egyptian reliance on fate and omens is provided by the fact that Masudi, writing fifty years earlier, had told a similar tale about Alexander's founding of Alexandria. The name al-Qahira, 'the Triumphant,' could have appealed to al-Mo'izz on its own merits.

4 This wide street has shrunk to a tiny portion of its original fifteen yards; a rather narrow lane, lined with later mosques and small shops stacked with pots and pans, its official name, Sharia al-Mo'izz, still recalls the first Fatimid caliph. As the main axis of Cairo from Fatimid to Napoleonic times, the street through which conquerors paraded, the link between the gates in the northern wall and Bab Zuweyla in the south, it is still known to

the people of Cairo as 'Bayn al-Qasrayn,' or 'Between the Two Palaces.'

7 SALADIN

1 *The Muqaddimah of Ibn Khaldun* (trans.). Ibn Khaldun died in Cairo in 1406 and was buried in a cemetery outside Bab al-Nasr.
2 H. A. R. Gibb, *Studies on the Civilization of Islam.*
3 Still visible as part of the Coptic Museum.
4 Ibn Jubayr used the term *Rumi*, from the Arabic word for Constantinople, the new Rome.
5 Karakush, Saladin's architect, may be the origin of Karagoz (literally 'Black Eyes'), the hero of the traditional Turkish puppet show.
6 Abdul Latif al-Baghdadi, *op. cit.*
7 AD 1196–97.
8 Marcel Clerget, *Le Caire.*
9 Lane-Poole, Cairo: *Sketches of Its History,* p. 191.

8 TREE OF PEARLS

1 Edward William Lane, *The Manners and Customs of the Modern Egyptians,* p. 446.
2 An example of the *mahmal* is preserved in the Ethnographical Museum of the Geographical Society of Egypt.
3 This custom was only discontinued in the twentieth century when the creation of Saudi Arabia, ruled by Wahhabite puritans, led to its suspension.

9 PLATONIC REPUBLIC WITHOUT PHILOSOPHY

1 D. Weil, *Geschichte der Chalifen.*
2 Sir William Muir, *The Mameluke or Slave Dynasty of Egypt.*
3 Lane-Poole, Cairo: *Shetches of Its History,* p. 95.
4 Mosque of Sultan Hassan, AD 1356.

10 MAMELUKE DAY

1 Muir, *op. cit.,* p. 15.
2 The mosque of this important complex still stands on the west side of Sharia al-Mo'izz. It occupies the site of a small Fatimid palace originally built for the sister of the caliph al-Hakim. Kilawun and his son Nasser are buried in the mausoleum.
3 These included a restoration of Ibn Tulun's great mosque.
4 Muir, *op. cit.,* p. 55.

5 The quarter near the old Roman fortress had retained a Christian character; to this day it is predominantly Coptic.

11 MAMELUKE TWILIGHT

1 They stand where Sharia al-Mo'izz bisects Sharia al-Azhar; the area is now known as al-Ghuriya.
2 Ibn Iyas, *Journal d'un Bourgeois du Caire* (Fr. trans.).
3 1514.
4 1461–1467.

12 MAMELUKE NIGHT

1 K. M. Panikkar, *Asia and Western Dominance.*
2 The Shakespearean term for Arabs.
3 Ogilby ignores the Islamic adherence to the lunar year, which causes the season of pilgrimage to process through the solar year.
4 Muslims would be horrified to hear that their sacrifice was offered to their Prophet, the burden of whose message was that God had no partners.
5 Emir al-Hag in the Egyptian pronunciation; the Commander of the Pilgrimage.
6 The Ottoman sultan. Only about this time was the Ottoman empire ceasing to be the major power in Europe.
7 The Citadel.
8 J. H. Rose, *Life of Napoleon.*

13 NAPOLEON THROUGH CAIRO EYES

1 Koran viii; 46.
2 The most prestigious collection of the traditional sayings of Muhammad.
3 Quoted in J. Christopher Herold, *Bonaparte in Egypt,* p. 15.
4 *Ibid.*

14 MUHAMMAD ALI & COMPANY

1 Charles Issawi, *Egypt at Mid-Century.*
2 "... d'un goût contestable mais d'une somptuosité folle"— Théophile Gautier. Later bought by a rich Coptic family, it became, in the 1960s, the Omar Khayyam Hotel.
3 Lane-Poole, Cairo: *Sketches of Its History.*
4 *Ibid.*
5 M. S. Anderson, *The Eastern Question,* p. 240.
6 Lane-Poole, *The Story of Cairo.*

7   J. W. McPherson, *The Moulids of Egypt*.

8   S. S. Hill, *Travels in Egypt and Syria*.

15   FIFTY-FIFTH CENTURY

1   The low-relief friezes in the Sakkara tombs vividly portray this agricultural seriousness.

Bibliography

Anderson, M. S., *The Eastern Question, 1774–1923*. New York, Macmillan, 1966.

al-Baghdadi, Abdul Latif, *The Eastern Key*. tr. Ivy E. Videan and Sayid Zand. London, Allen & Unwin, 1965.

Burckhardt, Jacob, *The Age of Constantine*. Garden City, N.Y., Doubleday, 1956.

Chennels, E., *An Egyptian Princess by Her English Governess*. London, 1893.

Clerget, Marcel, *Le Caire: Etude de Géographie Urbaine*. Cairo, 1934.

Creswell, K. A. C., *Early Muslim Architecture*. 2 vols. Oxford, 1932–40; also abridged, London, Penguin, 1958.

Cromer, Earl of, *Modern Egypt*. 2 vols. London, Macmillan, 1908.

Devonshire, R. L., *Rambles in Cairo*. Cairo, Constable, 1917.

————, *Some Cairo Mosques and Their Founders*. London, 1921.

Fattal, Antoine, *Ibn Tulun's Mosque in Cairo*. Beirut, 1960.

Frescobaldi, L., *Viaggio in Egitto e in Terra Santa*. Rome, 1818.

Gautier, Théophile, *Voyage en Egypte*. Paris, 1870.

Gibb, Sir H. A. R., *Arabic Literature*. Oxford, 1926.

————, *Studies on the Civilization of Islam*. London, Routledge & Keegan Paul, 1962.

Grünebaum, Gustave E. von, *Medieval Islam*. Chicago, The University of Chicago Press, 1946.

199

Haswell, C. J. R., "Cairo origin and development, Some notes on the influence of the river Nile and its changes," *Bull. Soc. Geog. d'Egypte*, II, 1922.

Herodotus, *Histories*.

Herold, J. Christopher, *Bonaparte in Egypt*. London, 1962.

Hill, S. S., *Travels in Egypt and Syria*. London, 1865.

Hitti, Philip, *History of the Arabs*. London, Macmillan, 1937.

Ibn Battuta, *Travels in Asia and Africa, 1325–1354*, tr. H. A. R. Gibb. London, 1929.

Ibn Duqmaq, *Kitab al-Intissar, Description de l'Egypte*, ed. Vollers. Cairo, 1893.

Ibn Iyas, *Journal d'un Bourgeois du Caire*, tr. and ed. Gaston Wiet. Paris, Librairie Armand Colin and S.E.V.P.E.N., 1955.

Ibn Jubayr, Travels of, tr. and ed. R. J. C. Broadhurst. London, Jonathan Cape, 1952.

Ibn Khaldun, *The Muqaddimah, An Introduction to History*, tr. Franz Rosenthal. 3 vols. Bollingen Series. New York, Pantheon, 1958.

Issawi, Charles, *Egypt at Mid-Century*. Oxford, 1954.

al-Jabarti, Abdul Rahman, *Merveilles Biographiques et Historiques*, tr. Chefik Mansour Bey and others. Cairo, 1890.

Lane, Edward William, *The Manners and Customs of the Modern Egyptians*. London, 1860. Reprinted, Everyman's Library.

Lane-Poole, Stanley, *Cairo: Sketches of Its History, Monuments and Social Life*. London, 1893.

———, *The Story of Cairo*. London, J. M. Dent, 1902.

Lange, K., and M. Hirmer, *Egypt: Architecture, Sculpture, Painting in 3000 Years*. New York, Phaidon Publications, 1967.

Lauer, Jean Philippe, *Sakkarah, Les Monuments de Zoser*. Cairo, 1939.

Leo Africanus (al-Hasan ibn Muhammad al-Wazzan al-Fasi), *History and Description of Africa*, tr. Pory, 1600. London, Hakluyt Society, 1896.

Loti, Pierre, *Egypt*, tr. W. P. Baines. London, T. Werner Laurie, 1909.

McPherson, J. W., *The Moulids of Egypt*. Cairo, 1941.

Madden, R. R., *Travels in Turkey, Egypt, Nubia and Palestine in 1824–1827*. London, 1833.

Maqrizi, Taqi al-Din, *Description topographique et historique de l'Egypte*. Cairo, Bouriant and Casanova, 1895–1920.

Marie-Carre, J., *Voyageurs et Ecrivains Français en Egypte*. 2 vols. Cairo, 1932.

Mayor, L. A., *The Buildings of Qaytbay, as Described in His Endowment Deed*. London, 1938.

Meinardus, Otto F. A., *Christian Egypt, Ancient and Modern*. Cairo, 1965.

Muir, Sir William, *The Mameluke or Slave Dynasty of Egypt*. London, 1896.

Muller, Max, *The Mythologies of All Races*, vol. 12. Boston, Marshall Jones Co., 1918.

Nasir Khosrau, *Sefer Nameh*, tr. Charles Schefer. Paris, 1881.

Ogilby, John, *Africa*. London, 1670.

Panikkar, K. M., *Asia and Western Dominance*. London, Allen & Unwin, 1953.

Pauty, E., *Les Hammams du Caire*. Cairo, 1933.

Rose, J. H., *Life of Napoleon*. London, George Bell, 1901.

Russell, Lady Dorothea, *Medieval Cairo and the Monasteries of the Wadi Natrun*. London, Weidenfeld & Nicolson, 1962.

Stewart, Desmond, *Young Egypt*. London, Wingate, 1958.

Volney, M. C-F., *Travels through Syria and Egypt in the Years 1783, 1784 and 1785*. 2 vols. London, 1838.

Webster, J., *Travels through the Crimea, Turkey and Egypt, Performed during the Years 1825–1828*. 2 vols. London, 1830.

Wiet, Gaston, *Les Mosquées du Caire*. Paris, Librairie Hachette, 1966.

Index

203